A

PRESA :S: PRESS

BOOK

P.O. BOX 792   ROCKFORD, MICHIGAN 49341

Books by Eric Greinke

Sand & Other Poems
Caged Angels
10 Michigan Poets (As Editor)
The Last Ballet
Iron Rose
The Drunken Boat (Translations from Rimbaud)
Masterpiece Theater (with Brian Adam)
The Broken Lock (Selected Poems)
The Art Of Natural Fishing
Whole Self / Whole World

WHOLE SELF / WHOLE WORLD

(QUALITY OF LIFE IN THE 21st CENTURY)

Eric Greinke, M.S.W. , C.S.W.

PRESA :S: PRESS

FIRST EDITION

Printed in the United States of America

ISBN 0-9740868-3-5

Acknowledgments: Thanks again to Roseanne and Anna. Without their efforts the editing and early production stages of this book would have been improbable.

Library of Congress Control Number: 20004100029
Cataloging Information: 1. Greinke, Eric, 1948-
2. Social Criticism. 3. Mental Hygiene. 4. Parenting.
Title: Whole Self / Whole World
Subtitle: (Quality Of Life In The 21st Century)

website: http://www.publishershomepages.com/php/Presa_Press
email: presapress@aol.com

Contents

Happiness and quality of life are largely determined by basic beliefs and attitudes. Better mental hygiene can be achieved through internal locus of control, divergent thinking, acceptance of reality, time competency, and examination of the basic beliefs that support these strategies.

Developing a truly universal perspective requires a new paradigm of the nature of intelligence. Anthrocentrism prevents us from recognizing the intelligence and rights of other species. Participation in universal society requires that we achieve peace on this planet, through individual growth.

Chapter One

Another Good Day To Die

A doctor chided his elderly patient: "You cough constantly from years of smoking. Your liver is shot from all your drinking. If you don't stop these bad habits, they're going to kill you!"

The old man laughed harshly. "Well, I pity all the health-nuts who end up dying of nothing!"

Quality of life is strongly influenced by the attitudes and behaviors of a person, and an awareness of death is the foundation of the positive attitudes and behaviors that increase quality of life. Every person is a microcosm of humanity itself, and the problems of society and of our planet can only be solved by improving the functioning of each individual.

Awareness of death brings perspective and clarity to life. It is the first great reality to which every other aspect of life is relative. Rather than being morbid, a constant awareness of death leads one to appreciate life more and function at a higher level.

Each of us needs to develop skills that minimize negative life experiences, and maximize positive life experiences, to optimize quality of life. There are a number of principles which may be learned and operationalized as life skills and practiced as mental hygiene. These skills are seldom consistent with the materialistic values that are predominant in society today. Each of the principles that lead to maximum quality of life are addressed in the chapters of this book. Illustrations are drawn from my own life experiences and from my observations as a human service professional. In this first chapter, the importance of developing a constant awareness of death is presented as the basic foundation one needs to develop high quality of life.

Death is the first fact of life. I became aware of the reality of death at the age of three. My family had gone to the beach at Holland, Michigan, for the day. The beach was close to our home and we went there frequently. Despite the fact that I did not yet know how to swim, my favorite activity was to float on an inflatable seahorse, up and down on the Lake Michigan waves. The waves would break into a row of white caps every 8-10 feet. I was riding happily on the seahorse. The waves and sky were a lovely blue. My parents were on a blanket on the beach, their attention on my baby sister, when I noticed that I was floating away from the beach. This is one of my clearest early memories, because of what the event revealed to me. I remember how pleased I felt, to be floating there, when suddenly a large wave knocked me over. I suddenly found myself hanging upside down in the water. I had the thought that I was going to die. My eyes were open, and I felt strangely detached as the bubbles rose around me in the blue-green water. I could see the seahorse above me, and the surface of the water, but I could do nothing but hang on. It was difficult to hold my breath. Then, I saw my father's feet and legs and felt his grip as he hoisted me out of the water. I clung gladly to him as he stood in what was, for him, waist-high water. They tell me that later I wanted to get back on the seahorse, but that they wouldn't let me. I remember that I realized that I could die. One didn't have to be an adult for it to happen.

The next time I caught a glimpse of death was at the age of eleven. I had two close playmates who were brothers. One was my age and in my classroom at school. He had a great sense of humor and was known among our group as quick-witted and funny. His brother was one year older and also a great guy. It was considered a bonus to be able to play with the brothers because you got the two-for-one effect. We always tried to gather as many kids as possible to play Cowboys and Indians, or War. We used to gather as many as twenty boys in the nearby woods, armed with BB guns, to play soldier. We had a vague idea that it was dangerous, but we didn't take the danger seriously. In the Fifties in Michigan, every boy had a Daisy BB gun, and wasn't afraid to use it. Boys did all kinds of dangerous things, protected by the false security of youth.

One day in late summer, I was going over to play with the two brothers at their house. Their parents were gone. Several of us were going to take our BB guns to the woods. We all loved to do this. All our fathers had "real" guns. When I got to the brother's house, I was shocked to see an ambulance in their front yard and two police cars in the driveway. A small crowd was forming on the sidewalk. A couple of other boys had arrived before me, and were crying. I learned that the brothers had been playing with their father's shotgun and that the younger had accidentally shot and killed his brother. I was horrified. I burst into tears and ran home. The boys in the neighborhood stopped playing with the BB guns for quite awhile. We also temporarily lost interest in trying to find and handle our father's guns.

The next day my friend was sent away to a home for emotionally disturbed children out in Colorado. He missed the sixth grade completely, and when he returned for the 7th grade,he was no longer the funny, happy person I had known. He was sad, and seldom smiled or laughed. Once, when we were in the 8th grade, a 10th grader called him "killer" at a pep assembly, and my friend burst into sobs right there. After school that day a mutual friend fought the 10th grader over it and beat him mercilessly.

When the shooting happened, I realized how abruptly death can change everything, and how precious life is. I made a conscious vow to live every day as if it were my last. How could one ever know that he might live another day?

The next year, at the age of 12, I lost my paternal grandfather, one of my favorite people. He died of boredom. He was healthy as long as he worked, right through retirement. When he first retired, he went around the neighborhood fixing things for people. After a year, he had fixed everything in the neighborhood. He was too efficient for his own good. He'd always been an intense worker. He'd always been in charge, popular, a glad-hander and joke teller. He loved action. "He ran out of things to do, and then he died." said my grandmother.

My next experience with death came at the age of 14 when the boy across the street died at the age of 16 from a brain tumor. This boy was always mean to me and bullied me for a year until I'd had enough. I nearly killed him by hitting him over the head with a steel pogo stick, resulting in a concussion and 19 stitches. The brain tumor was discovered about a year later and he was hospitalized for 3months before he died. I always wondered if the blow I'd given him contributed to the brain tumor and his death.

Once again, I was profoundly affected by the reality of death. All of these incidents reinforced the vow I had taken to always live each day as if it were my last. I also realized that my interactions with another person could have a profound effect on him, or even threaten his very life.

Death is the great reminder. It reminds us that time is all we've really got. Quality of life can be greatly affected by our attitudes and behaviors. Quantity of life is a complete unknown. One can only be alive in the present moment. Death is the great reality that makes life precious.

When we really recognize the reality of death and its unpredictable nature, we understand that there is no time to waste on activity that does not produce the highest quality of experience available at any particular moment. To maximize the quality of each moment is to experience *more life*.

If you were informed that you had a terminal cancer and had but one month left to live, you would want to "live it up". Quality of time becomes a major issue when death is near. Yet, none of us can know that he will not die today. Death is *always* possible, lurking just around the corner. It seldom gives fair warning.

When I was a sophomore in high school, I had an older friend named Art Lewis who was in the senior class. We had two Sociology classes together, and he and I always led the class discussions. We both enjoyed sociological subjects. We also had in common that we both were much taller than the other students. He was on the varsity basketball team. I liked his thinking and his eloquent speaking style. He had a lot of warmth and wasn't too busy to talk to underclassmen like me. I was deeply hurt when he was killed in Vietnam the year after he graduated. He was a great guy who lived less than a year after high school. Art

11

was one of many, in those days.   The year after high school graduation, I lost several other good friends in Vietnam. Each of these friends was special to me, and I mourned each loss.

Upon graduation from high school, at the age of 17, I enlisted in the U.S. Coast Guard.   I had many life and death experiences as a member of Coast Guard Search and Rescue Teams.

It seemed we always had to go out on a Search and Rescue mission when the sky was the darkest, the waves the highest, and the wind the strongest. On the night I'm going to tell about, it also rained. One moment a Coast Guardsman can be sleeping in his bunk and the next he is pulling on his boots and foul weather gear.   Within minutes we were charging out to a black, towering sea, hanging on to the boat as it bounced violently. On this particular occasion I was standing next to the mast, holding on to it with one hand. Suddenly we hit an out-of-sequence wave, about a 10 footer, and the boat ploughed into the trough between the waves with a shuddering crash. The large brass bell on the mast above my head broke off and, barely missing my head, broke through the deck right by my foot, embedding itself into the marine- grade 3/4" plywood deck. I could have been killed by that bell.

Moments after my arrival at my first duty station out of boot camp, three of us tried to breathe life back into a 5 year old boy who had drowned in Lake Superior. We worked long and hard at it, but finally had to admit it was hopeless. On any given day a Coast Guardsman might see death. There is always a good chance that he will be killed or injured. I learned to wake up every day with the thought that this day could be my last. This became a lifelong habit. It is not a morbid preoccupation, but rather a reminder that time is important and that quality of life needs to be a constant concern. Every day should be Thanksgiving and Valentine's Day. Everything we do counts. If an awareness of the fragility of life is nurtured and maintained, all life experiences are greatly enhanced. A sunset is more beautiful to a person who *realizes* that it could be his last.

On another occasion, after an exhaustive search, we successfully rescued the pilot of a small plane that had crashed into Lake Michigan about 15 miles out. While we were attempting to tow his plane back, it began to sink. We had to cut the tow line. The pilot became irate and began to shout about the financial value of the plane. Finally, the Boatswain's Mate informed the pilot roughly that he was lucky to be alive. While he did stop shouting and complaining, I don't know if he really understood the predominant reality. Many seem to think they'll live forever, but their attitudes are unrealistic. They waste precious time on materialistic and other trivial concerns, because they don't recognize the fragility of life.

My father once told me to never do anything that I would not want to be caught dead doing. An awareness of death is a basic building block of a responsible existence. When the implications of such an awareness are carried to their logical conclusion, they affect one's moral values profoundly. No one knows that today will not be his last day of life, yet so many people seem to put off dreams and experiences to a tomorrow that *truly* may never come.

Real and dramatized violence and death on television and in movies desensitize people to death's reality. Our senses become numbed by the constant bombardment. Life is cheap in the Third World and on television. The great humanitarian Dr. Albert Schweitzer wouldn't step on an insect because his regard for life was so strong.

Materialism is no protection or comfort in the face of

death, and yet materialistic concerns seem to prevail. When Thoreau wrote that "the mass of men lead lives of quiet desperation", he was referring to the tendency of people to live lives that do not satisfy them. Materialism is a dead end street. Not only can't you "take it with you", but materialism puts an emphasis on quantity rather than quality, in having rather than *being.*

Spirituality and materialism are diametrically opposed. When one becomes focused on counting possessions, one never has enough, by comparison, to what one does not have. When material concerns are de-emphasized, however, appreciation of time, surroundings, relationships with others and with nature, is stimulated. Every moment is special when one truly appreciates life's fragility and unpredictability. Wonder and peace return to one's life when material concerns are placed in proper perspective.

One needs to ask if the cost-benefit ratio is positive or negative for any given activity. The value of one's time should always be considered. Remember where time comes from: your life. What is your life worth? Not much, if you waste your time.

My great-grandmother Sorenson was a very active 103 when she died. She was a swimmer her whole life and had a daily swim up to a week before she died. She and I fished together frequently when I was a child. She loved to talk and knew what joy of life is. She liked to dance and danced well past the age of 100. Dancing through a century was her idea of living a high quality life.

When I worked at a long term care facility for elderly, a freshman in college and straight out of the Coast Guard, I had old men tell me goodbye on two different occasions, and predict that they would die that night. Both times I went into work the next day to find that the person had actually died as he said he would. I guess they could feel it coming.

I witnessed the deaths of numerous elderly people in the years I was a Geriatric Orderly. The basement of the facility was filled with body bags when the Hong Kong Flu first hit the country. Elderly patients with weak constitutions were dying at the rate of several a week during that epidemic. When the first crude vaccine was brought out, it actually killed numerous elderly persons before a weakened version was brought out for children and elderly people. At one point, in a facility that held about 150 patients, we had ten corpses in the basement. The mortuary wagons rolled in and out all that day.

It's been over twenty years since my father's death, but I still miss him. Sometimes I imagine that he is an angel watching over me. His life and death taught me the importance of following your dreams.

My father was a great lover of music and exhibited musical giftedness at an early age. By the age of 10 he was an accomplished accordion player and by 12 he was playing in his father's Chicago dance band. When he graduated from high school, he was awarded a scholarship to a music college, which his father "let" him accept only on the condition that he also apply for a Tool and Die Apprenticeship, as he felt that music was a poor choice for a career.Dad started at music school after sending an application to General Motors Institute first. His grades were excellent and he was very happy at the Hager School of Music when the Tool and Die Apprenticeship came in. He was submissive to his father's wishes and quit music school to become a Tool and Die maker, and this became the turning point of regret in his life. That decision to go against his heart's desire ultimately killed my father. It began as a small sliver might in your finger, working its way in deeper until a cyst forms around it, and grows to press on a nerve until the finger hurts all the time and finally the whole hand is compromised.

Before his apprenticeship was completed, he was drafted into World War II. He went to Europe, landing in France and fighting all the way to Berlin, with the Army Tank Destroyers. He saw his best friend killed, and later I was named after the friend. Upon return, he completed his apprenticeship and became a Tool and Die maker at General Motors. He married my mother in 1946 and I was born in 1948, eldest in my generation. My sister was born two years later.

Father was unhappy working as a Tool and Die maker. He played his music every chance he got, but he didn't like being an amateur. He could play several instruments, and continued to learn new instruments throughout his life. When my Great-Grandpa died, he left my Dad his violin, an instrument which Dad had never learned to play. Dad took the violin into his little music room and came out 2 hours later and played us a piece beautifully.

My parents divorced when I was 6 years old, which is a kind of death in itself. When a child's belief that his parents are in love is shaken, it becomes a search for love that might last a lifetime.

My Dad remarried about a year after my parents were divorced. He was happy for a while with his new wife. My half-brother was born when I was 10. When I was 19, my Dad and his second wife were divorced. By this time, he had slipped into depression about his life. It was existential angst, a general feeling of disappointment, dread and hopelessness. He wished his life had been different, but he'd lacked the initiative and self-confidence to make it so. People loved his sensitivity, but he was actually hypersensitive. My

16

stepmother told me that she still loved him, but couldn't live with him because of his unhappiness.

His drinking began in earnest when he divorced his second wife. I was just out of college, married 3 years, the first time I intervened. I arranged for him to get treatment at the Veteran's Hospital in Battle Creek, Michigan for a few months, then he moved in with my wife and me. At first he was much improved, but after we moved him to his own place again, he steadily slipped back into drinking. Being alone was very hard for him. Two years after the first intervention, the cycle repeated itself. He went back to the Veteran's Hospital, moved back with us, did fine, then fell off the wagon as soon as he was by himself again. We were expecting our first child, and I was in graduate school and working full time as a social worker by then. I neglected to check on Dad for about a 3 month period. When I did check on him, I was horrified at what I found.

Every flat surface in his apartment - windowsills, shelves, even the floor, was covered with empty wine bottles. In the middle of the living room was a chair, and stacked next to the chair were numerous spiral notebooks. The wine bottles numbered in the hundreds, and surrounded the chair.

I told him that he needed to go back to treatment, and he agreed to go on the next day. I became insistent that he leave with me *right then*, and he refused. I told him that I was pouring the remainder of the current bottle in the drain right then, otherwise I was washing my hands of him. He looked at me defiantly and said "Go, then." So I did. I walked out and didn't see him for about 4 months, until the night I watched him die.

I was working at a group home for emotionally disturbed children and was called at work by my brother, who informed me that our Dad was in a coma and wasn't expected to live through the night. He'd collapsed on the street with a heart attack.

When I got to the hospital, they were all gathered around his bed. My sister just happened to be on a rare visit to Michigan, or she wouldn't have been there. My half-brother, barely out of his teens but a father himself, stared tearfully at our dying father. Dad was hooked up to a respirator and an IV and he looked 84 instead of 54. His feet stuck out at the foot of the bed and his toenails were long and yellow.

When I walked in, my brother moved away from the head of the bed. I stood by my father and his eyes opened. He gazed into my eyes for a long moment, then his eyes rolled up and he died. My brother and sister broke out in tears. I did not. This happened 10 days before my first child was born. The night my eldest son was born I went home alone and cried for both the death and the birth all night long.

At the funeral, I was amazed at the large number of people. Several people whom I didn't know came up to me to tell me how Dad had helped them when they'd needed it.

At one point during the visitation, my grandmother and I sat on a loveseat away from the main crowd. She had lost her only son, her first-born. She said "You look more like your father than ever before. It's in your eyes." She did not know that I had been looking into his eyes when he died.

I was the executor of my father's "estate". When we divided his personal effects, the only thing my sister wanted was his accordion. My sister hadn't heard him play since she was 5 years old. So, she needed the accordion. My brother and I divided Dad's personal things between us. I took the 30 notebooks of writing and my brother, who had mechanical skills, took his tools.

When I read through the 30 notebooks, I was struck by

their range. Some of it was brilliant, filled with minute, personal observations of life. Other parts were absurd, paranoid, filled with anger or self-pity. I burned the notebooks in a pile in my backyard.

My paternal great-grandparents died within moments of each other, despite being in two distant wings of a large facility. They had immigrated from Germany as young adults. Great-grandma spoke no English, and as they got into their late seventies, she became senile. She used to become confused about who people were. She variously thought that my Dad was my Grandfather, that I was my Dad and that my Grandfather was his father, her husband. She thought she was still back in Chicago. When Great-grandfather could no longer take care of her, they moved together into the local Lutheran Home. He used to visit her in the afternoons, but lived in a ward of ambulatory and lucid male patients. On the day she died, Grandfather, who *had* been in excellent condition, had a sudden heart attack within moments of her death. No one had told him she died. He must have felt her die, after so many years of marriage.

In my 25 year career as a clinical social worker for children I have often experienced the deaths of children. Some were killed because they persisted in high risk behaviors. Some were severely developmentally disabled, dependent their whole short lives on machines to eat and to breathe. I have seen situations where literally millions of dollars have been spent to extend the lives of children who could not breathe or eat on their own. Speech, hearing, physical therapy, occupational therapy and nursing care were all provided to kids who ultimately died before reaching school age. One of the workers in our agency lost eight children in a matter of a few months. The other workers, employing "black humor", nicknamed her 'The Angel of

Death'. She finally couldn't take it anymore and quit for less stressful employment. One can only tolerate so much reality.

It was generally known by the social workers, doctors, nurses and other professionals that most of the severely disabled children would die within a year or two. It was our job, therefore to increase the child's *quality of life* for as long as it lasted.

When my stepfather died his cat let out an unearthly howl at the moment of his death. Twenty miles was the only thing that separated them. I was the last person to see him alive. He fell asleep while I sang the old folk song *'500 Miles'* to him.

We have all lost friends and relatives whom we loved. Death is ubiquitous. Those whom we love move from our outside lives to our inside lives.

Although it is inevitable, death is nothing to be afraid of. There are only two possibilities, neither of them frightening. If consciousness continues after death, then in effect, there is no death. If, on the other hand, consciousness ends at death, there is nothing to be afraid of. The frightening thing is to have never really lived.

Quality of life depends on valuing each moment. The many opportunities for new and special experiences that are potential in each moment are often missed by those who 'forget' that life is fragile. The future is a delusion that often keeps us from living fully.

Too many people wake up to 'just another day', when each new day is really another good day to die.

Chapter Two

The Zen Of Love

Once we thoroughly digest the fact that we are fortunate to be alive, the question of *quality* of life arises. Love motivates, validates and gives meaning to our lives. Without it, all the material wealth in the world will not produce quality of life, and with it, one truly needs little else.

Even basic survival is tied to love. Abraham Maslow, Ph.D., attempted in his work to establish a "hierarchy of needs", in which he assumed physical survival to be the most basic need of all. Maslow failed to conceptualize that love is actually a matter of *degree* and that even physical survival *presupposes a degree of love* that is a-priori to survival itself. The first level of love is self-love. Without a measure of self-love and valuation, one has no desire for physical survival. Physical survival requires a will to live, and a will to live is dependent on a measure of self-love and valuation.

A depressed person, clinically defined as one whose anger is turned inwardly, becomes immobilized and often unable to care for himself. His physical health, as well as every other aspect of his life, declines along with his self-concept. He perceives himself as undeserving of quality life experiences or circumstances. Those of us who are in the mental health professions are quite familiar with the syndrome presented by depressed clients whose self-loathing causes them to repeatedly set themselves up for rejection by others. They truly feel that they deserve rejection, failure, even punishment. A popular song from the Sixties went: "Only love can break your heart. Only love can mend it again." Although love may seem abstract, it has very real physical manifestations.

Self-love is necessary in order for love of others to develop. Children learn to love by being loved. Love gives children the ability to act positively, and develop social skills.

Love is the strongest of the human emotions. But it is *not essentially an emotion* in the sense that it's popularly perceived. It actually begins with a thought, and the emotional aspect of love is secondary to it's rational foundation, which is *respect*.

The ground-breaking psychologist, Albert Ellis,Ph.D., the Gestalt therapists and the vast majority of psychologists and therapists of recent years all recognize that emotion is secondary to thought. To put it simply, one cannot have a feeling that is free-floating, relative to no-thought. If we dig deeply, we find that feelings are always *about thoughts*.

Positive thoughts lead to positive feelings. Conversely, negative, irrational thoughts lead to negative, irrational feelings. Therapy would have no value if it weren't for the truth of this basic principle. As it is, we are able to help people to reconsider their basic beliefs and attitudes and show them how their happiness and general quality of life are tied to their thinking errors, because emotional problems are caused by negative thoughts, beliefs and attitudes. *Love is defined as respect combined with affection.*

Being in love is a special state of awareness wherein one's ego-boundaries are expanded beyond the self. Self-love is obviously a precondition for *being in love*, as well as for survival itself.

Being in love, at its highest level, is a state, rather than an action or reaction, wherein one's level of involvement with the object of one's love is central to consciousness and which colors all action and subsequent thought and feeling with positivity and strong desire to express joy, kindness, respect and affection outwardly.

Rollo May, Ph.D., in his book *Love and Will*, contended that love is inextricably connected to will and is the culmination of all positive action as well as it's source. In an existential sense, love is synonymous with life itself, as the basic element of a desire to live well and meaningfully. In a very real, non-abstract sense, the Beatles were right when they sang "All you *need* is love". (Italics mine.)

The human need for love is so great that all human behavior can be traced and linked to it. The linkage is considerably easier to conceptualize and observe when one bears in mind that love exists in *degrees*. When a person acts in a way that others perceive as cruel, evil or anti-social, it is always because the person's love needs have been deprived and frustrated. Some people are needier than others, and may have a need for love that is so deep that normal amounts and degrees of love cannot fill the deep-felt void. Entertainers and others who crave public adoration are an example of those whose love needs are greater. Sometimes they have experienced actual deprivation, but sometimes not. They may have a genetic predisposition toward neediness, and/or lack a basic understanding of how to achieve a consistent and satisfying level of self-love and self-esteem. It is common for those who feel deprived of love to seek love-substitutes.

Criminals and those with personality disorders, whose love needs were deprive
identification with others that is the basis of a conscience. They cannot "see" beyond themselves, and need to compete for love and its substitutes. Money is primarily a love-substitute, as is fame. Those who seek and desire fame and fortune have decided that actual love is not forthcoming or available to them, and so they become adept at procuring substitutes. They do not realize that love is not a commodity that can be pursued. Rather, it is a *state of being* from which joy and meaningfulness *ensue*.

The Christian Bible says that "God is love." Jesus said "love your brother as yourself." The converse meaning of the "Golden Rule" is to do to others that which one wants done to oneself. Thus, the relationship between self-love and love of others is clearly stated in Judeo-Christian theology.

The Buddhist idea of emptying oneself of desire is also related to the achievement of a state of *being in love*. When desire is gone, true appreciation and joy of life and ego-expansion ensue.

Because love is the highest state of being, it is blocked by competition, selfishness and greed, which result in a tightening of the ego-boundaries rather than the expansion of boundaries characteristic of the state of *being in love*.

We achieve wholeness through love, because it is its own reward. Love is felt as love is given, completing the circle. It is at once the act of a whole person while it also produces and reinforces that very wholeness. Experienced as an emotion, it has its origin in thoughts of respect, admiration and appreciation. It is the ultimate act of thanksgiving, the ultimate expression of joy of life. It brings the best out of a person and also opens a person up to the fullest appreciation of life.

The two words go together: life and love. The often asked question "How's your love life?" might be shortened to "How's your life?"

Love is not desire, but an appreciation of what is. It fills a person with such satisfaction that desire disappears. Desire is the craving for love, and is resolved when a state of being in love is achieved. Love must be achieved, as it cannot be merely obtained.

Love of nature opens up a person's perspective, allowing him to see that he is not the center of the universe, but only a small speck of life in a universe that is infinitely alive. This form of love leads eventually to spirituality, the essence of which, universally, is the state of oneness with the world, the total expansion of the ego to identify with the whole natural world. This may seem terribly abstract, but it is actually the failure of individuals to achieve spirituality which results in hunger, wars, and the destruction of the environment.

Love has its own inherent morality, the natural knowledge of which exists within every heart. Loving actions reinforce themselves, and everyone who really loves knows the difference between actions that are loving and those which are not.

And yet, despite its power to transform lives and ultimately the world itself, real love is rare. In his book, *The Art of Loving*, Erich Fromm, Ph.D., explores the barriers to real love in great detail. His position is that expansive love is rare because it is the act of a whole person and people aren't complete because they are deprived of love as children. In short, Fromm felt that most people are generally too mentally unstable, neurotic and damaged to participate in expansive love.

25

The role of the mother is particularly significant in the development of a capacity to participate in love. In a developmental sense, the mother teaches the child to love by loving the child unconditionally. The child's sense of well-being, of self-worth, and ultimately, of the joy of life comes from mother-love. When people lack trust and maintain a suspicious, hostile view of the world, it indicates a disturbance in the mother-child love relationship. Studies have shown that a child who is not cuddled and held during the first year of life usually loses the capacity for intimacy. Those parts of the brain that correspond to intimacy and closeness to others actually atrophy when deprived in early infancy.

As a social worker for emotionally disturbed adolescents, I observed a strong correlation between cold, detached mothers and disturbed children with low self-esteem.

It is not unusual in today's world for babies to be signed up for day care prior to even being born. This is a trend which my wife and I have observed too often in the child care program we have operated for the past fourteen years. Babies in this situation bond primarily with the day care provider rather than with the actual parents. They are commonly left in day care for ten or eleven hours a day, five days a week. When they are handed over to their natural mothers at the end of the day, they often cry and fuss. When this happens I cannot help but note how earlier in the day, during their most active period, they happily cooed, smiled and blew bubbles, looking lovingly into my wife's eyes while she held them and fed them their bottles.

If the world is becoming a more hostile and selfish place, perhaps the correlation between mothers working during the first few years of life should be more seriously examined. Can society really afford it?

Single mothers, whose numbers have increased exponentially, often spend the greatly diminished time available to the child by attempting to be both father and mother, a grave error where the child's emotional development is concerned. The role of the father is distinctly different from that of the mother, and involves a more conditional response which serves under normal circumstances to socialize the child. As such, the father's role, though equally important in the final analysis, is dependent on the mother's, which provides the foundation upon which the personality is built. The most elaborate, well-built building will not stand if it is built upon a poor foundation.

A person who experiences maternal deprivation is like a house of cards, in an emotional sense. When the winds of trauma and life's challenges hit him, he crumples and falls. This is reflected in rising divorce rates, substance abuse, domestic violence, child abuse and neglect, animal abuse, alienation, rootlessness, prevalence of personality disorders, insensitivity to the plight of the poor and homeless, destruction of the environment and the general perception of a low quality of life.

The decrease in maternal skills and concerns is symptomatic of a heartless society, as well as its ultimate cause.

Being in love is the closest thing we have to heaven on earth. Jesus said that in order to enter the Kingdom of Heaven, one must enter as a little child. A childlike openness to experience is a primary goal of Buddhism.

Many people feel that love is hard to find, because they look for it in the wrong places. Love is not a commodity to be obtained, and cannot be found in the world. Love must be sought inside one's self. It is an ability, an act of will and a choice. Most people retain at least some degree of a capacity for love, although it may not be enough to produce a love that extends far into the world. Fixations on love substitutes, such as sex for its own sake or material consumption are far more common than a real connection with the love-energy that will result in a true joy of life.

The ability to love rests largely on acceptance of surface differences. One must see past cultural, gender, racial, even species-based differences to identify with other persons. Those who feel themselves deprived by comparison to others are not likely to overcome the perceived differences, as one *must* do to love. All living beings have more in common than they have *meaningful* differences. Every animal on the planet values life and wants it to continue. Whether we have four furry legs or two bare legs we share the same desire to live as well as the same basic emotions.

Peace is an outcome of love. We do not have world peace because we do not have world love. Scarcity of resources and the huge gap between the haves and the have nots is both a reflection and cause of war, international conflict and hatred. This is *not* abstract!

Hatred is the polar opposite of love and as such they are inextricably connected. Hatred is caused by deprivation of basic needs. It is a response to threats, real and imagined, of loss.

Anger is denial of reality, and an expression of hatred. Anger and hatred are denials of love and peace. Peace comes from acceptance of things that cannot be changed, courage to change that which can be changed, and the wisdom to know the difference, to paraphrase the Serenity Prayer used in twelve step programs and in the universal morality that is common to all the major world religions.

There is, indeed, a universal morality, which is a natural outcome of man's inherent capacity to love. If each person were capable of being in love with life, living love, we would not need criminal laws. Our negativity is so prevalent that such a statement is regarded as an impossible fantasy of an Utopian nature, yet, it is completely true and greatly to be desired, and it is the ultimate key to the long term survival and evolution of the human species, the planet, and the other species who live here with us.

It is direction that counts, not velocity. If we head in the direction of love, we might eventually get there. If we head toward further divisiveness and conflict, both internal and external conditions can only deteriorate further, until our systems eventually collapse like a proverbial house of cards. If selfish, short-sighted greedheads continue to damage the environment for personal "gain", eventually, none of us will survive. Love is the key to survival of the human race and of the planet, no less. Just because it is abstract does not mean it isn't a very real factor in our survival. Love is the *primary factor* in achieving and maintaining quality of life, for each of us and for all of us.

Love multiplies. It does not divide, though many feel that there is only so much to go around, so they get it backwards.

Humans have been emotionally deprived for so long that it has become the norm. Cynicism and generalized hostility and alienation are so common that love's truth is questioned and ridiculed and rejected out of hand as naive, other-worldly and absurdly unrealistic. Yet, humans are actually obsessed with love, as reflected in popular entertainment and culture. Love figures prominently in novels, movies, songs and poems, and is the essential value of the world's religions. Love is a great mystery to people, yet they do not attempt to study it formally, or even think about it seriously. Love is the missing link when it comes to man's understanding of man.

Indeed, pessimism and cynicism are great barriers to love, and sex adds to the confusion. Many equate sexual attraction with love, as the strong pleasurable feelings allow one to engage in an *act of love*. There are many acts of love, but none are so immediate and intense to the average person as sexual interaction usually is. Sometimes, only self-love is glimpsed through sex, but at least it's a start.

During great sex, the persons involved are giving and taking simultaneously. Loving acts of all kinds have this *simultaneous reciprocity* in common. A loving act is its own reward.

Sex therapists tell us that when sex is bad, it is because a connection has not been made. When one or both parties are focused only on personal pleasure, it is not an act of reciprocal, mutual love. But even so, there is a large measure of self-love, which is the first level of love, involved even in selfish sex. Thus, sex is easily confused with love, and when the average person is asked how his love life is, he interprets the question as "How is your sex life?"

The prevalence of sexual imagery in our culture is symptomatic of our increasingly desperate hunger for love. The Greek word eros is translated as a love of life. "Erotic" originally meant a *celebration of life* rather than sex. Its use today is exclusive to sex and sexually stimulating imagery. A beautiful nude is erotic, but so is a beautiful flower, or sensuous music, or anything that is life-affirming or contributes to a joy of life.

Time provides a structure for life, and love provides quality content within that structure. Love energy can outlive an individual lifetime. Time and love define each other, as two sides of the same coin. Love can multiply itself. A beautiful painting continues to give love long after the artist is dead and gone. A mother who deeply loves her children multiplies and concentrates the power of love energy that can live on past her own mortal life. Love is the gift that truly keeps on giving.

It is not naive to say that we need more love in this world or that love can solve the world's problems. This is not the same as making a grandiose, idealistic statement that is impossible to obtain, because *it is possible to achieve,* and indeed, if it is not, there is literally no hope for our planet and those who live with it. It must be achieved by individuals, however. Political and social engineering cannot, by itself, solve the world's problems.

Humans already have a universal moral code, but deviation from it is so widespread that we have become pessimistic and untrusting of it. All human cultures have universal taboos, according to the anthropologists, such as the taboos against incest and murder. Universal taboos reflect the inherent morality of love, which is cross-cultural and unchanged by time.

Murder is virtually unknown among animals other than man. If an animal kills another of its own kind, it is unintentional. When two wolves, baboons, lions or deer fight over a mate or a territory, for example, one usually surrenders once the dominant one is recognized, and the submissive or defeated one is allowed to skulk away. *If* each person was in touch with the power of love that is inherent in every human heart, there *really would be no need* for a law against murder or other violence. Love and morality go together. Love is related significantly to not only morality, but to death, to time, to quality of life, to meaning, to our survival, to the environment. Love is the key to human potential. It has been said that we only use ten percent of our brains. What percentage of our hearts do we use? Our evolution as a species has gone through the technological revolution, and the new frontier is the moral and spiritual development that we need for survival and real, meaningful progress.

Love has power when it is *believed in*, at the deepest level. In order for love to exist as a core belief, it is best established during a child's formative years, when basic beliefs about reality are formed. Attitudes and behaviors are secondary to basic, core beliefs. Love can move mountains, and achieve great things, when it is coupled with faith. One needs to trust in the power of love for it to have life-changing power. Such trust and faith generally only come from formative experience. If a child consistently experiences love, he learns to trust it, and a foundation for a joyful and loving life is established. Here, again, the relationship between time and love is clear. Children need time to learn that they are loved. Adults seem to largely believe that children assume they are loved, and this is far from true. Adults are focused on quality of time, whereas time has less meaning to children, and they need repeated, consistent demonstrations of love in order for them to gradually develop a concept and an understanding of love. If we want children to develop the moral value that love is the most important thing in the world, we must recognize that children learn gradually and need a tremendous number of repetitions to glean meaning from their experiences. Adults are working off an experiential baseline. That is much easier than the initial development of an experiential baseline, which is the task of childhood.

The needs of children must be reconsidered more carefully in the light of current cultural and lifestyle trends, and those trends that lead to deprivation of basic childhood needs, such as absent fathers, mothers working during the first five years of life, media violence, increased materialism and technology, and decreased interaction with the natural world. These need to be re-evaluated for their impact on the personality development of children and adolescents. The social problems of the next few decades will come from the children of today. If we want to prevent those problems, we must address their causes. If we can eliminate most of the anti-social feelings in the children by recognizing and meeting their emotional needs more effectively, we can greatly diminish the social problems of the immediate future within one generation. Meeting children's true emotional needs requires a new set of priorities from adults.

Adults must recognize that children are more emotionally fragile and dependent than we generally realize. The power of parental love will be our greatest asset in changing society, once the true nature of childhood becomes common knowledge. I have worked with neglectful, abusive, substitute, and well-meaning natural parents in parenting support groups and therapy groups for thirty years, and I truly believe that most parents do the best they can, based on their knowledge. Improving their knowledge has almost always resulted in improved functioning as parents. Most parents love their children, but they simply don't understand children well enough to provide the childhood experiences that children need to become loving citizens of the world. The world cannot be whole until the people in it are whole. It all boils down to individuals, and can only be changed on an individual level. The world will be whole when the individuals in it are whole.

If love brings the best out of an individual, it follows that it also could bring the best out of large groups of people. The current trend of "political correctness" is a clumsy, but well-meaning attempt to apply the universal morality of love into specific social situations, attitudes and policies. At certain points, the clarity of universal morality breaks down, and moral debates arise, such as that over abortion, which polarizes people and makes the loving solution hazy. Each side of the debate is focused on a different love-object, pitting the rights of potential mothers against those of potential children. Love has an answer for us, but we must be more loving to see it. The answer will be found in the heart, when it is finally found, and the greatest good will eventually be the standard by which the solution will be judged.

Being deeply in love with my wife has had more impact on the quality of my life than any other factor. Love multiplies when one is deeply in love. I love her more every day. As my appreciation of her grows, so does my capacity for love and for positive action.

Love nurtures and causes one to nurture. I am a better father and citizen because I love and am loved. The more I love my children, the more I love all children. The more I love, the more I live. These statements are not mere abstractions, nor are they meaningless cliches with no meaning in the 'real' world. Far from it! Love is at the very core of all positive value and meaning. It is the basic positive principle in life. It is a mountain within which there are deep, rich veins of gold, waiting to be mined, the greatest natural resource of all.

Chapter Three

The Karma Of Materialism

Most people would agree that there is a strong relationship between quality of life and the material world. In general, people seem to consider materialism in a mostly positive light, but in my view, people do not usually notice when their materialism reaches the point of diminishing returns. I am referring not only to personal possessions, but also to the structures that support them. One sure way to lower one's quality of life is to waste time working at employment that is meaningless. Meaningless, unfulfilling employment occurs because a worker has decided to trade time for money, based on a perceived need and also on a belief that a more meaningful option is unavailable. How many people would keep their jobs if not for (perceived) financial need? They keep their eyes on their bank accounts, bills, and financial goals, but ignore the clock which keeps on ticking toward their deaths.

I live with my family across the highway from a large, spring-fed lake. When we moved here nineteen years ago, about 25% of the lake was undeveloped woodland, and about half the dwellings on the lake were small seasonal cottages, averaging $50,000 to $70,000 in monetary value. At this point, 19 years later, there are no woodlots remaining and every lot on the lake has been built on. There are no seasonal cottages left. All of them were extensively remodeled, second and sometimes third stories were added, and the homes are now ostentatious year-around houses valued between $250,000 to $500,000. Ironically, they are empty most of the time, as their "owners" are out working to pay their huge mortgages. Their children come home from school to a large, empty house, or go to day care. Despite the fact that there are expensive boats docked in front of the houses, there is no boat traffic during the weekdays. The boats stay at the docks while the houses are used primarily for sleeping and to house lonely dogs all day long. On weekends, the boats buzz frenetically around the lake in big, clockwise circles, the "owners" hurrying to take advantage of their limited "free time".

The great Canadian philosophers known as "Loverboy" have stated that "Everybody's working for the weekend." and I believe they are largely correct. Out of a week, two days are available for personal pursuits while five are devoted to selling, manufacturing or manipulating plastic trinkets, car parts or perhaps computers. Common experience is marked by non-personal goals and activities. Time is strictly scheduled, while energy is expended on tasks and concerns that do not satisfy one's emotional, creative or spiritual needs. Indeed, these non-material needs begin to recede into mere dreams, and finally atrophy, leaving the dreamer bereft and possessed of an undefinable yearning and existential dread.

The vacuum is finally all they feel, and they try to fill

it with more stuff, more materialistic "solutions" that, like any addiction, merely fuel greater desire. Fame and fortune are seen as the collective ideal. Self-satisfaction, based in a love of life, is unknown to all but a few.

There is an inverse relationship between materialism and creativity. Creativity arises as a response to situations of low resources, where inner resources awaken to adapt to the situation. Children are creative with basic toys like blocks, balls, and figurines. When a technologically advanced toy is activated and placed in front of most children, they watch it for awhile, and soon lose all interest in it. Most children start to become cranky soon after they begin "playing" with an electronic toy, a toy that essentially plays with itself or plays for the child. We have noted, in 14 years of providing day care for children, that building blocks are unanimously preferred as the most popular toy, day in and day out. Outdoors, a simple ball is the most preferred toy.

There is also an inverse relationship between materialism and spirituality. Jesus said that it would be easier for a camel to pass through the eye of a needle than for a wealthy man to enter heaven. A wealthy man expressed a desire to follow Jesus, and Jesus told him to give away everything he owned if he wanted to follow him. Jesus felt strongly that spirituality and materialism were incompatible modes of being. He admonished others not to build up treasures on earth, where they could be stolen by thieves or deteriorated by the elements, but rather to build up inner, spiritual riches. Ironically, most of the churches established in his name are quite materialistic. Jesus drove the money changers from the temple, but the Christians invited them back in. The lilies of the field notwithstanding, the vast majority of people seek wealth and material possessions with all their energy, and consequently sell, rather than smell, the roses. I think they do smell the coffee, however, because they drink an awful lot of it.

Spiritual riches cannot be categorized nor counted. Increasingly, people reflect the amoral values of their computers, and computers can only count, categorize, and quantify. They trade away their souls for instant gratification and more "information", but the *quality* of the information is greatly diminished.

Spirituality is incompatible with goal seeking. It cannot be sought, but must be let in, or accepted. It cannot be controlled.

There is yet another value which has an inverse relationship with materialism: emotion. I don't mean that people don't become emotional over money, possessions, and status. They obviously display and experience the lowest of emotions in this regard, such as greed, jealousy, resentment, and hatred. It is the positive, life affirming, altruistic, humanistic, loving feelings that are squelched and strangled by over-concern with materialism.

Is all materialism bad? A certain degree of it is necessary for quality of life. A dwelling is one possession that can enhance quality of life significantly. By and large, the homeless do not lead quality lives. Every animal has its own dwelling. Only humans wander homelessly against their wills. The problem arises when the cost of the dwelling reaches the point of diminishing returns. When a person labors all day at a meaningless job merely for money, to support a house which stands empty most of the time, a monument to the occupant's ego and a projection of the occupant's desired social status, it becomes a dysfunctional relationship. The house owns the occupant. He works for it, and it is a pitfall he can't climb back out of, because his priorities are backward. He ends up wasting his time,

forgetting that time is all we really ever have. He would be better off with a smaller house and more free time. Perhaps then he could work at employment that he truly enjoys. One should never work just for money or status. If you do, you are a wage-slave.

The Beatles, among other songwriters, have noted that "Money can't buy me love", and it's true. Love is the greatest factor in quality of life. If a man wants to feel enriched, he'd be better off learning to love a dog, a child, or a woman, than having many dollars. Truly loving another being requires a different kind of effort, but the rewards are emotionally infinite. A life without love is a poor life indeed, whereas, if you have love, material needs are greatly reduced and placed in a more realistic perspective.

Love brings out the best in a person, whereas materialism brings out the worst. It is said that love of money is the root of all evil, yet this formulation appears to inspire little serious consideration by the majority, who are more like the fabled lemmings, blindly following blind leaders until all are in over their heads, drowning in despair.

Materialists do not like to consider the inequities of the world. They become so intensely narcissistic that they consume way past the point of need while other people starve and go homeless within a short distance of their personal castles and hoards of mostly superfluous stuff. Their greed has made them truly decadent, wasting precious resources for mere amusement,while the vast majority of the people on this planet live in perpetual political and economic crisis,starving, or running for their lives from their burning homes,their dead left behind. AIDS is an epidemic in Third World countries. Millions of people are sick and dying while the affluent few don't even realize how fortunate they are, but feel themselves to be greatly deprived because they have not met all of their personal financial or career goals. They lack awareness of a universal consciousness that allows them to relate to mankind as a whole.

Because they are not whole, the world is not whole. We work at cross-purposes between ourselves, our environment and each other, because evil greedheads don't see beyond their own desires. The narcissist feels that the world exists for his convenience and revolves around himself. Other people are like furniture to a narcissist.

Historically, as the industrial revolution developed into the technological revolution, people have become increasingly mechanical and computer-like. Experience does alter personality. In the post-WWII years, the personality of the time was seen as primarily neurotic. Karen Horney wrote *The Neurotic Personality of Our Time* to identify and explicate the phenomenon.

In the Eighties, Christopher Lasch identified the American personality as narcissistic, in his book *The Culture of Narcissism*. Both books were bestsellers, and both were successful in identifying the cultural and sociological factors that influence the development of personality types within the context of history.

Psychologically, a neurotic personality has higher functioning than a personality disorder. As a personality disorder, the narcissistic personality is primitive and lacks an ability to relate to the needs of others. Neurotics, on the other hand, feel guilty if they don't consider the needs of others, to such a degree that they are fraught with anxiety, guilt and regret. Neurotics have overdeveloped consciences, whereas a narcissistic personality lacks any true conscience.

The need for instant gratification is a narcissistic personality trait that has been greatly reinforced by our growing dependence and fixation on mechanical and technological experiences. Not only are we what we eat, but we become shaped by what we do and how we spend our time. The computer has speeded up or eliminated many processes that used to reinforce human creativity, expression of feeling and spirituality. Pure research done in a library, using books and other printed material, reinforced the values of patience, persistence, critical thinking, aesthetics and creative hypotheses. Today, all a researcher needs to do is type in a subject, press 'search' and press 'print'.

Jesus said that no one could "serve both God and money". He said that where your time was spent, where your thoughts were, determined where your heart was.

Other world religions have also identified the conflicting values inherent in materialism and spirituality. Zen Buddhism, Taoism and Hinduism all emphasize the simplification and minimalization of one's relationship to the material world.

As noted previously, materialism becomes negative when it passes the point of support, and causes the reverse effect: the person becomes the supporter of the material "possessions" that then *own him*, cause him to waste his time, and to focus on meaningless values such as status, obsessive collection of objects large and small, and greed. Objects are not substitutes for love, joy and peace, yet they are pursued as if they were.

One of the common symptoms of an emotionally starved, narcissistic, materialist, is the habit of collecting. The object collected becomes a symbol of what the collector really wants and needs but doesn't know how to get. Most of the time the collector is fixated on the object collected due to an association with an early experience of feeling loved and valued.

The collector tries to fill the inner vacuum created by

41

his materialistic lifestyle instead of recognizing its effect and changing the lifestyle itself. Caught up in a vicious circle, the materialist has eliminated from his life those very sources of strength which would empower him to improve his quality of life. Many have forgotten (or never learned in the first place) how to value each moment of life or express love. They do not know how to structure their lifestyles in a way that enhances their quality of life. They accept materialistic, self-defeating values without critical consideration, assuming that the values of the majority must be right.

Mutual love does not arise from a relationship that is based on the objectification of persons, based on the person's materialistic value (income, looks, wealth). Materialistic considerations are rocks and weeds in the garden of love. Love survives *in spite* of a degree of materialistic concerns, not because of it.

Materialism also interferes with the development of a healthy sense of self. By eliminating all extraneous possessions from one's life, a person learns to prioritize and to stop being concerned over the trivial and superficial. Not only do materialists judge the worth of others by external standards, but they also judge themselves by them. A healthy self-concept cannot be based in what one has. It must be based on what one is.

A person is freed from slavery when each aspect of his relationship with the material world has been scrutinized, and eliminated when found to be superfluous. Again, a house is usually needed, because it enhances one's quality of life in several ways. Conversely, a huge, ostentatious house that is primarily a status symbol, costing more than a person can afford (both in money and time), is often the basis for an unbalanced relationship with stuff, a dangerous pitfall not easy to escape. Materialistic priorities are bad Karma.

Conspicuous consumption is embarrassing to all of us - it identifies the consumer as frivolous, self-indulgent and lacking in social consciousness. Anyone who doesn't think of the have-nots and the doomed, needs re-education in humanism at the very least. Those who do realize that they are wasting resources while others are starving, homeless and sick, but do it anyway, are doing *evil*, not only to others but to themselves as well. They are experiencing life in an externalized way, rather than internally. Their orientation is to events and objects in the external, material world, often to such a degree that their inner world becomes barren.

The Karma of materialism is that the more stuff one has in the outside world, the less one has inside. Conversely, the more one simplifies and downsizes one's relationship with the material world, the more one develops inner wealth.

Decisions made in major areas of life such as type of employment and housing, have a major impact on quality of life, with less often being more. Personal possessions also have a major impact on experience and require self-discipline and accountability if one is to get the most out of life.

My own relationship with stuff has been a great emptying-out process and has helped me to clarify and prioritize my values. I have always been intrigued by eliminating superfluous possessions. At this stage of my life, I own fewer personal possessions than at any point, yet feel wealthier.

When I was an adolescent I collected many books, art supplies, clothes, sports equipment, musical equipment, and even statuary. When I went into the Coast Guard I learned that not only could I live out of a sea bag, but that I enjoyed it. Just a sea bag and a guitar case was all I needed to pick up and move 400 miles to a new station. Walking through the spruce forest of Michigan's Upper Peninsula, I carried whatever baggage I needed in my pockets, and felt enriched and full. If, conversely, one's focus is on material concerns, then the ability to appreciate the subtle "best things of life" that are free, atrophies.

The point of diminishing returns occurs at that point where objects or activities own you. Sometimes a possession no longer justifies its existence because it isn't used. The criteria I use centers around two principles: (1) low cost/benefit ratio and (2) low or no usefulness. Both are aspects of the principle of diminishing returns. There are many options in major life choices that produce the 'more for less' effect. A low cost/benefit ratio, where the cost is low but the benefits are high, is often the result of choosing an option that the majority of people would not even consider. If you do what you've always done, you'll get what you've always gotten.

People become hung up on particular things, always to their own detriment. Owning a particular thing never makes a person smarter, nicer, more noble nor happier. In Zen Buddhism, one renounces desire to achieve a state of bliss. By emptying the mind and heart of petty, material concerns one is able to experience life more directly.

Each individual needs to find a comfortable relationship to the external, material world, to enhance quality of life. The important thing is to examine these relationships consciously.

Of course, it would be a mistake to obsess over stuff even in order to overcome its control and influence. One needs to find a relationship with stuff that is optimal and comfortable, so that the degree of materialism supports, rather than diminishes quality of life.

I have been acquainted with two "poor little rich boys". It has been fascinating to observe how they have dealt with the situation of being born into wealth and power. Both refused to take over lucrative, international family-owned businesses, and sought lives that were non-materialistic. One was a teacher, then a race car driver, and a poet. Eventually he wrote and published several well-regarded novels. The other 'poor little rich boy' became the executive director of a philanthropic organization he developed, using his share of the profits from the family business. He liked to associate primarily with poets, artists and social workers.

Anyone can benefit by reassessing the degree of materialism in his life. Some may not be aware of efforts to impress others, and may need to ask themselves if they would still function the same way if there were no others to impress.

Once a reasonable, albeit subjective, relationship with materialism has been conceptualized, a person needs to focus on streamlining. Down-sizing and streamlining are two concepts from business that are helpful in achieving personal control over material concerns. For example, once one has determined how much house is optimal for him, for positive reasons that support one's freedom and the meaningfulness of one's lifestyle, then it is valuable to focus on completely owning that house as soon as possible. Statistically, only one percent of American homeowners own their homes outright, with no encumbrances. This is a pitiful statistic, and surely proves that animals are smarter than people! Most people make the mistake of buying expensive, big-ticket 'toys' such as boats or second or third cars, various recreational vehicles, or going off on expensive vacations. Most of these would not be needed if they were better organized and considered the cost/benefit ratio. If the money that is diverted into these pitfalls was put on the principal of their home loans, people could pay off their home in one-third the time, saving tens of thousands of dollars in interest, gaining time, and giving themselves and their families better security.

I think that people often fail to assert their real existential needs when they buy a house. Surroundings are a large factor in your experience of life. It is certainly a completely different experience to be poor in the country than in the city. I know 'poor' people who live like wealthy country squires, hunting and fishing on their own property and relaxing in the privacy and peace of a rural environment. I know others with the same level of income who live in urban environments fraught with crime, blight and social tension.

More people are moving away from urban environments to improve their quality of life. In most cases, it actually costs less to live in the country than in the city, which brings me to a final important point: when one develops a sensitivity to the distinctions I have noted, the ability to choose and develop situations wherein you get *more for less* becomes heightened and honed. One learns to get more out of life, through quality control.

Getting one's relationship with stuff straight is one of the most difficult tasks of modern life. It is an area where people tend strongly toward conformity, and seldom analyze the situation for themselves. People have a strong tendency to buy things which they really don't want, influenced by advertising, media and other external pressures. The negative side of the thing is usually not discovered until it has already been purchased and allowed into one's life.

Often the person has a fantasy of what the new item will do for him, and either the reality is not equal to the projected fantasy, or the effect of the item is to consume more time and space than anticipated. If a person were more devoted to really thinking ahead about the new item, or hobby, or experience and its potential cost, he could avoid a lot of waste.

For example, Michigan has the highest per capita boat ownership in the country, due to our many lakes. The vast majority of these boats are unused nearly all of the time. Nearly every house has a boat sitting in its yard that hardly ever gets moved or put in the water. Used boats are for sale on every street, indication to me that people often imagine that they will use a thing, but they really don't know themselves. They like the idea of boating better than actual boating. The person who can avoid these pitfalls through careful situational analysis and self-awareness can redirect his resources to more meaningful priorities.

One should always consider not doing something from a beneficial standpoint. Quite often, when we have the impulse to get something or to do something, we haven't considered whether we'd be better off not getting it or not doing it. By actively criticizing and questioning our own impulses, our actions become more considered, responsible, efficient and honest. We can counteract them in cases where the impulse is revealed to be a poor choice. Conversely, if the impulse turns out to be a good choice, it will not be the worse for becoming a thought-out action. Any action that is positive can bear up to scrutiny, whereas the negative actions reveal their faults under thoughtful consideration. It seems rather simple, but I have learned, as a psychotherapist, that people seldom question their own impulses, preferring to act out feelings, which often results in undesired outcomes. Curbing one's own impulses in general, and in the area of materialism, in particular, leads to improved quality of life.

Another thing I have learned as a therapist is that people seldom know what they really want. My job as a therapist involves helping my clients to see themselves more clearly. Plato said "know thyself", and psychologically, that is the best advice, though that doesn't make the task easier.

The primary barriers to self-knowledge are dysfunctional values, beliefs and attitudes. Materialism is often a response to scarcity of resources, a big factor in the human condition. Statistics on obesity show that the lowest on the socio-economic scale are also the fattest. Presumably, poor people eat more out of emotional neediness, the same reason wealthy people collect possessions. Their emotional needs are only exacerbated by their attempts to satisfy themselves. Perhaps they would do better to consider that a radically different approach to the problem could be more successful.

It is unfortunate for the planet and for the human race that society, as a whole, reflects the shallow, selfish values of the individuals in it. Social problems exist on an individual level. They are 'seen' as wider social problems, but this is really just a way to conceptualize the effect of many people dealing with similar psycho/social situations in similar ways.

Materialistic concerns, whether by 'choice' or 'necessity', do not bring out the best in human beings, to put it mildly. By creating a situation that gives basic support to the individual, we can create a world that is more equitable, less threatening and more nurturing.

We need to develop global awareness. In one sense, an *ego-boundary* is a zone around a person that is self-identified as self. It may be conceptualized as an invisible circle around a person. When a person feels threatened, and lacks self-confidence, the ego-boundary shrinks. In extreme cases, persons with psychoses become alienated even from their own bodies (i.e. Catatonia, Disassociative Schizophrenia). Shrinkage of the ego-boundaries occurs when a person feels overwhelmed, alienated and threatened by reality. Many distortions of reality may then be manifested, seemingly beyond the person's control. There is a vast literature devoted to this phenomenon.

What of the opposite state, where the *ego-boundaries expand*, beyond the self? When we love our children, for example, we have expanded our invisible circle to include them. Vicarious pleasure in a loved one's pleasure is actually greater than experiencing direct pleasure for oneself. Being in love is a state of expanded ego-boundary. Identification with the person loved must be strong for this to happen.

If a person dearly loves plants, for example, it is not much of a leap for that person to become active in efforts to save the forests. Since plants need water, this person expands his boundaries to include a concern for global water quality. This *concern,* in turn,leads inevitably to action in the material world.

If global consciousness was understood to be a more valuable goal than selfish personal materialism, global peace would then be at least possible. The greatest barrier to peace, throughout world history, has been the endless competition over territory and material resources.

It is vital that we recognize and identify that the great barrier to world peace is runaway materialism. An unwillingness to share limited resources denotes a world filled with people who generally have narrow ego-boundaries, poor identification with fellow humans and with the planet.

We tend to perpetrate the values we are taught in our formative years, both directly, by our teachers and parents, and vicariously, through observation of our families, culture and environment. As adults, we need to learn to think divergently, to question the materialistic values we have taken for granted. We also need to learn how to transmit positive spiritual, emotional and creative values to our

49

children, to create a generation that is devoted to inner peace and to peaceful interaction with nature and fellow man.

The positive value of materialism should be seen as relative. It is only positive up to the point of diminishing returns, and the returns are not all material. The non-materialistic aspects of life are the real riches that can lead to a life of high quality for each of us, and ultimately, for all of us on this battered planet.

Chapter Four

The Technological Prison

Technological developments have such far reaching effects on society and culture that individuals are unable to escape. Our personal freedoms and options have become so circumscribed by runaway technology, that, compared to the first two million years in the history of our species, we are virtual prisoners. The cultural effect of technology is so all-encompassing that it is difficult to know where to begin.

Historically, the development of the printing press was probably the first significant technological development to have widespread effects on the way we functioned both personally and as a society. The printing press made several things possible for the first time. Instead of books being produced by hand, one at a time, for a small minority of literate clerics, books could be mass produced. Mass production of books had enormous positive effects, and perhaps a few that were not so positive in the long run.

Mass production of books gradually set off a powerful change in society. The ideals of Democracy, which included freedom of speech, the press and religion, were all ultimately spread through the technology of the printing press. Without the invention of the printing press, there would have been no record of Shakespeare's plays, no Protestant Reformation and no Renaissance. The invention of the printing press had a seminal effect on world culture and literacy, and marks the beginning of an extremely powerful force, that of mass production technology, that had an enormous effect on man's social evolution.

Darwin could never have disseminated his theory of evolution had it not been for the printing press. Ideas became incredibly more powerful when replicated in print for anyone to read. It was the very existence of books and print that made it possible for ideas to have such power, regardless of the actual content of the books. Ideas that were so widely disseminated, quality notwithstanding, gained the power of multiplication, a power that was unknown and nonexistent prior to the technology of the printing press. Many of the ideas thus empowered by mass production and dissemination stimulated great social change and conflict. The pen became mightier than the sword when the printing press was invented. The whole direction of social and individual evolution was altered by this one invention. Most of us would agree, that in the case of the printing press, the widespread effects of technology were positive. Yet, there was also a downside, hardly noticeable at the time, in the shadow of the positive effects of this technology.

Ancient religions, a belief in magic, oral traditions, wide cultural diversity, powerful secret skills and knowledge of all kinds was destroyed by printing technology. Ideas that were in print became so powerful due to mass production, that they greatly overshadowed those ideological, religious and philosophical systems that did not find their way to print. In other words, when we gained something through technology, we also lost something that was perhaps equally valuable.

The ancient European religions were destroyed by the spread of Christianity. These ancient religions were nature-based. People related to fertility cycles and to the seasons in a very personal, spiritual and respectful way. The first book ever printed was the Gutenberg Bible. Without debating the relative value of Christianity, it is easy to see that the ancient Teutonic, Nordic and Celtic religions had no chance of survival, because the Christians had the advantage of technology. Later, the established and powerful Roman Catholic Church was itself to feel the power of the printed word, in the writings of Martin Luther and the Protestant Reformation that followed. Technology has a way of backfiring on those who rely on it. One of the earliest English novels was *Frankenstein* by Mary Shelley, in which the tendency of technology to create unexpected monsters is the theme. Technology often bites the hand that feeds it. If we, as a species, had not developed the use of fire, we might not have survived. Today, however, the internal combustion engine threatens to deplete the planet of fossil fuels that took billions of years to formulate, fouling our atmosphere, increasing the global temperature and bringing us to the brink of an environmental apocalypse. We have wars over oil and we are dependent on technology that has widespread, unexpected, negative consequences.

We all learned in American history class how the invention of the cotton gin forever changed a way of life in the South and led to the American Civil War. The entire South became impoverished because of technology. This is not to say that slavery was good, but only to give another example of the widespread social and cultural effects of a technological development.

It isn't always the 'bad guy' who is the loser. Books themselves, which started the whole mass production trend, are slowly but surely being replaced by the electronic media. People watch many times more videos than they read books today. Literacy has been negatively affected by television. The vocabulary of a young person today is far smaller than that of the pre-television generation. Words represent ideas. Today's less literate youth has fewer ideas to work with. They are more homogenized, less individualized and less creative.

The fate of nations has been ruled by technology, and the history of the world and of our species has been unequivocally altered by technological developments. Wars have been won because one group or nation had better technology. A club was no match for a sword. A sword was no match for a musket. A musket was no match for a repeating rifle. The second World War was ended because the Allies developed and used the atomic bomb first. Today, the very existence of nuclear weapons is a threat to every single person, animal, and plant on the planet. A new technology always looks good at first, and later, when it is too late, its negative potential and effects are discovered.

The history of any human endeavor can be seen through the technological developments in that endeavor. When Sophocles wrote a play, it had to be experienced, in person, by an audience. When George Bernard Shaw wrote a play, one could read it before seeing it, or *instead* of seeing it, radically altering the dramatic experience. With the advent of radio plays, the visual was temporarily removed from drama. The visual came back, greatly altered, with television, which greatly decreased social interest in going to live stage plays. Movies took us into outer space through special effects, and made the unreal commonplace experience, while concurrently de-emphasizing and even replacing acting. When music videos were developed, music itself was de-emphasized and visual appeal overshadowed it. Technologies are cannibalistic. Long-play, vinyl, monaural record albums replaced gramophones and 78 RPM records, then were themselves replaced by stereo long play albums, which were replaced by 8-track cassettes, which were replaced by cassettes, which were replaced by C.D.s. At each juncture, something of value was also lost, if it didn't make the cut.

Only a small percentage of the music of the 20th century has survived to C.D.. Fewer and fewer titles are sold to more people, having a homogenizing effect. Anyone older than 40 knows how difficult or impossible it is to obtain favorite musical recordings made prior to the 1990's. It is even difficult to obtain literary classics today that were readily available twenty or thirty years ago. The vast majority of small, privately owned and operated bookstores have been driven out of the market by big, nationwide and world wide chain-stores. Today, publishers drop books from their lists unless they have big profit potential. The literary quality of a book is inconsequential in the publishing world if its profit potential is deemed low or marginal. He who controls the mass mediums of communication controls thought itself, to an increasing degree.

The overall effect is a narrowing of thought and an atrophy of the ability to think creatively outside of the parameters of the majority. We have increased literacy at the expense of literature, and also increased functional illiteracy concurrently. Students know how to key 'search' and 'print', but fewer of them know how to use a library, how to read critically and how to develop original ideas. Passive 'learning' has become the norm. Immediate gratification has replaced the ability and desire to defer gratification, because of technology. This is significant, because the ability to defer gratification is seen by developmental psychologists as a major factor in the development of personal maturity and success. Socially, an unstable economy is one result of the inability of *individuals* to defer gratification.

The more we rely on machines to think for us, the less human, and more robotlike, we become. As our world has been taken over by computers and our reliance on them, the downside is rearing it's head. As a society, we never seem to anticipate the full negative impact of any technology prior to embracing it. Even if the environmental impact is studied, it is inadequate and overshadowed by the excitement of the anticipated positive effects of a given technology. The social effects are *never, ever* considered. The effect of a technology on the personality development of individuals is absolutely never considered, when a new, revolutionary technology appears. Yet, the negative side-effects of technology are often socially devastating. Often, we have lost more than we gained from technology, as a society. The negative social changes are gradual, and so they go largely unnoticed in the heat of enthusiasm for a new technology, until it is too late, and the world has been transformed, downside and all. Today, individual privacy is being gradually eliminated by computers and electronic monitoring devices, yet the few protests that are voiced are ineffectual and largely unnoticed. Everyone accepts the loss of privacy as inevitable, and this becomes a self-fulfilling prophecy.

Quality of life is greatly affected by technological trends, and not always in a positive way. Mass production is so powerful, that individuals feel helpless, imprisoned by forces seemingly beyond their control.

We are like the lemmings that rush en masse to drown in the sea. We line up to buy cellphones and pay the price of diminished privacy. We drown in a sea of 'information'.

The technologies interact with each other, often to disastrous degree. Cellphone use while driving has created a new kind of car accident. Billions of dollars a year are lost through computer crime, a category of crime that did not exist before computer technology and the development of the internet. The internet spreads socially negative information as efficiently as it does prosocial ideas. At last count there were over 10,000 pornography sites on the internet. Racist hate groups communicate via the internet. Recipes for bombs and drugs are available to anyone in the world with a computer, via the internet. We in the mental health profession have noted the growth of a new kind of addiction, to the internet.

When personal computers were introduced, it was predicted by their manufacturers that paper use would decrease, saving trees. Instead, paper use has multiplied by tens and continues to rise. Technology changes so quickly that computers become obsolete in two or three years. Discarded keyboards and monitors have become a major source of lead pollution, negatively impacting soil and water. Computer and cellphone users are exposed to constant low-level radiation, the long-term effects of which are unknown. Neck and carpal tunnel conditions have increased dramatically due to computer use, even in small children. Visual problems are also increasing, due to hours spent staring at computer monitor screens and televisions sets. Obesity has become a major public health concern.

Car accidents are a major cause of death. People no longer work in the same communities in which they live, because of cars. The development of the automobile eventually led to the deterioration of the cities and to the development of suburbs. Suburbs grow at the expense of woodlands and farmlands, increasing levels of carbon dioxide and monoxide in the atmosphere while concurrently decreasing oxygen levels by cutting down trees. Yet, the technology for more environmentally friendly automobiles has been suppressed, due to the financial desires of a few entrenched greedheads.

There is a general, fatalistic belief that established technologies cannot be altered or eliminated. Technologies *can* be eliminated, with great difficulty. The difficulty is often based in economic forces, which seem to have a life of their own. Technologies can also be replaced by better technologies.

It took only 15 years to create a nuclear arsenal that was so huge that it was enough to kill every living being on the planet three times over. Hermann Kahn, in his book *On Thermonuclear War*, published in the early Sixties, wrote that the U.S. nuclear arsenal alone had an overkill factor of three. Disarmament has been so gradual that it is still not completed after forty years since the overkill factor was *noticed*, in the Sixties. The nuclear buildup only took one-third the time that disarmament has taken, *so far*. In the meantime, Third World nations have acquired the technology, making it questionable whether a worldwide nuclear disarmament will ever be achieved.

One nuclear accident and resultant chain reaction could easily cause the end of the human species and others besides. Technology often bites the hand that feeds it. An ounce of prevention is better than a pound of cure. Hindsight is good sight. Better safe than sorry. Look before you leap.

Electric lights are considered a great miracle of technology, and today we are dependent on them. Yet, medical science has found a correlation between artificial light and significantly lower sperm counts worldwide. Sleep disturbances and the production of vital light-related hormones are also correlated with the widespread use of artificial light..

In 1978, I reviewed a well researched, documented book for *The Grand Rapids Press* entitled *Four Arguments for the Elimination of Television* by Jerry Mander. Mr. Mander's arguments were not primarily social, but medical. Although his arguments against television were legitimate, they have gone unheeded, because of the universal denial of television addicted consumers. The book was widely regarded as Quixotic, despite it's factual accuracy, because television had become such an integral part of our culture and our lifestyle that no one could imagine life without it.

People love television so much that I wonder why this book was even published, despite its careful research and documentation. The very idea of eliminating television is more Quixotic than jousting at windmills, no matter how good the arguments. We have truly become the prisoners of the technology of television.

Mander wrote that total elimination of television is necessary because its faults are inherent in the technology. He presented evidence that television significantly lowers both intelligence and creativity quotients. Watching television is sensually limited to a flat, two-dimensional visual surface and a narrow range of sound, resulting in a form of sensory deprivation. As a result, viewers lapse into a passive learning state. Biofeedback studies have documented that no one can resist this effect for longer than twenty minutes of television viewing, after which brain waves slip into the same state as when we are dreaming.

While we are in this passive learning state, the television programs sell a way of relating to the world which emphasizes materialistic values and ignores moral values.

The paradox is that an inherently sensually-deprived experience is also addictive.

Biologically, the human eye is capable of transmitting approximately 18 images per second into the conscious brain. Television shoots images directly into your eyes at a rate of about 40 to 60 per second. Anything slower would be technologically impossible, or the projected images would not seem to move. Thus, most of the material enters the subconscious brain directly, without critical choice, there to influence and shape the values of the viewer beyond his conscious knowledge or control. Mander compared watching television to sleep-teaching and hypnosis.

The technology of television requires a high contrast of images due to its two-dimensionality. It therefore has an inherent bias toward gross action and away from subtle movement. Superficial pageantry and violence are better suited to the medium than sensitive aesthetics or rare details. Technical events, such as changes in camera angles, happen numerous times per minute, to keep viewer interest. The viewer is bombarded by imagery into a senseless, non-critical state, making television the most influential advertising medium of all time. Since its popular acceptance, the post WWII generation relates more to a bionic man than to a Einstein, Bernstein or Thoreau. As surface replaces substance, people become standardized, hypnotized and plastic automatons.

Mander further cited evidence that the light from television is physiologically harmful, producing brain tumors in laboratory animals and hyperactivity and attention deficit disorders in children. Unlike ambient lighting, such as that from a light bulb, television light is forcefully directed into the eyes by cathode rays. Our eyes have not evolved to accommodate such a barrage. The light makes you passive at the same time that the images make you hyper. The technology of television is too efficient as a teaching machine. It allows programmers to bypass your critical, conscious brain and program your subconscious brain.

In other words, television is brainwashing. This accounts for the fact that no one paid any attention to Mander's book. He presented us with a truth that we didn't want to hear. We were, and are, too addicted to consider the elimination of television.

Today, we are similarly addicted to computers, despite mounting evidence of their numerous negative side-effects. People who choose not to have personal computers are considered by those who do as have-nots and functional illiterates. The question of whether or not information-inflation produces a higher quality of life is seldom, if ever, posed. How the instant gratification of information at our fingertips affects our ability to think has not been considered. Lemmings don't think. They just follow their leaders over the cliff and into the sea..

All technologies, no matter how beneficial or exciting they appear when they are first introduced, have serious negative side-effects. I propose that we, as a society, begin to seriously consider the potential negative side-effects of any technology *before* implementation of it. We need to recognize the social and psychological impact of technology, as well as its impact on the environment. We need to ask how the new technology is likely to change our quality of life, in both positive and negative ways.

We cannot survive the juggernaut of technology unless we develop sanctions and systems to control it. At this point in history, quality of life is largely the issue. In a few short years, due to the exponentially increasing velocity and development of technology, it will be the physical survival of our species that will be at stake.

The millennium panic over Y2K is an example of technological short-sightedness. Somehow, an event that was only forty short years away was overlooked by computer developers. An ounce of prevention is worth a pound of cure. The cure, in this case, cost billions of dollars and created unprecedented worldwide stress. Never put all your eggs in one basket.

We already have alternative, environmentally friendly technologies, such as wind and solar power. We need to do much more to change over to them. We cannot afford the internal combustion engine anymore. Major, severe weather events, caused by global warming, are directly linked to the burning of fossil fuels by internal combustion engines and by factories. The link between materialism and technology is obvious. The economic environment needs to be managed on the basis of what is good for individual quality of life, for what is pro-social and for what is good for the environment.

An individual should not let his material possessions own him. Neither should a society let its technology own it. We must come out of denial, and face the reality of negative technological side-effects. They are much more far reaching than mere economics.

Technologies can imprison us, or help us. We must become more conscious of their impact *before* implementing them. A true understanding of the dual nature of technology would mean fewer life-altering negative side-effects. A truly responsible society would not allow any technology to be implemented prior to a serious, intensive study of its potential side-effects in all areas, including how it would impact on personality development and on health.

On a microcosmic level, an individual should not jump on any technological bandwagon until the negative impact on his quality of life is assessed. The impact of a technology on one's children should be a priority for any parent worthy of the name, otherwise we are not different from the lemmings, who apparently don't look before they leap.

I believe that if the human species survives, it will have to develop this consciousness and take these measures. It is only a question of when and how. The greatest barrier to the development of global consciousness is individual passivity and apathy.

Let us take a lesson from Dr. Frankenstein. When we think we are changing the world for the better, we often only make matters worse. Dr. Frankenstein wanted to create a superman, but the particular person he created had emotional needs that the doctor, in his enthusiasm for medical technology, failed to anticipate. The story of Frankenstein is an allegorical illustration of how technology has unexpected, negative side-effects, despite our good intentions.

Materialism and technology have led to the de-personalization of the individual. De-personalization has led to alienation, apathy and widespread narcissism. How can we realize our mortality, harness the power of love and avoid the pitfall of materialism in the face of these forces?

In the previous chapter I have noted that mental health experts denote narcissism as the dominant personality of our time. The evidence that this is so is all around us. Narcissism is a primitive personality disorder. Like all personality disorders, it is the result of the deprivation of a basic human need. Narcissists are detached and alienated from others and have an unrealistic and exaggerated preoccupation with themselves. They have a grandiose sense of self-importance and exaggerate their own talents and achievements. They focus on the special, unique nature of their problems, while exhibiting a cool indifference toward the problems of others. They have fantasies of unlimited love, power and success and react to the indifference or criticism of others with rage. They feel entitled to special treatment, but don't reciprocate. They take advantage of others for their own self-aggrandizement. They lack empathy and an ability to understand how others feel. They feel aloof and disconnected to others. Interestingly and sadly, this is precisely how Americans are as a group viewed by Third World nations.

These symptoms are caused by the deprivation, in childhood, of the need to feel special and loved. Parents who are narcissistic themselves cannot relate to their children and often substitute for loving attention by giving children material things. They use the television as a babysitter. They are too preoccupied with their own concerns to give attention and time to their children. If a parent is unable to consider the emotional needs of his own child, he is certainly incapable of considering the needs of future generations or 'foreigners'.

With the trend toward both parents working, and the rise in divorces, children simply do not receive the time they need with their parents in order to feel valued and special. There is no substitute for time spent with a child. It is a basic need of children to spend time with adults who love them.

Depersonalization also causes alienation from others and the over-emphasis of the self that is narcissism.

Depersonalization of the individual is caused by a combination of factors. In an industrial society, it is difficult to feel like anything but a number. Mass production work becomes meaningless, alienating blue-collar workers. Direct human contact is replaced by email and fax, alienating and isolating white-collar workers. A person's social status is based on what he does, rather than what he is. One is predominantly identified as a categorical type, rather than a unique individual. In adolescence, a developmental period of intense insecurity and narcissism, teens identify with and are identified by their peers, with groups. A teen can be a jock, a nerd, a preppy, a slacker, a punk, a stoner or a goth, to name a few of the current categories. Each of these labels serves to objectify the individual, subordinate to his assigned group identity. They then don uniforms to signify their group identities. In our youth-oriented culture, many people can not progress beyond adolescence. They just get older. They go from preppy to doctor or lawyer. Nerds automatically become computer programmers. These are materialistic labels that objectify individuals, based on a number, their yearly salaries.

Desensitization is another part of the process of depersonalization, alienation and narcissism. We are desensitized to human tragedy by the endless bombardment of violence and disaster on television. The line between fiction and non-fiction is blurred, and we become desensitized to death, violence and to the pain of others. Imagery is becoming increasingly sensationalistic, 'pushing the envelope' of violence.

Women are objectified by the media as mere sex objects. Racist stereotypes are constantly repeated, and individuals are seen first as members of their racial group, less and less for their specific individual qualities. Advertising and television manipulate imagery to sell material goods. The technology of television, using 40 to 60 images per second, directly projected by a cathode ray into your retina, puts the brain in a passive learning state. Critical assessment of the images and the materialistic values they represent is impossible because the human brain can only process a maximum of eighteen images per second. The television is too efficient as a programming tool. We were not evolved to deal with it. It literally imprisons our minds, first capturing them, then programming them with commercial, materialistic values. We become human automatons, and the basic need each person has to be an individual is alienated. Narcissism is a response to this deprivation, which is perpetrated by technology.

We become numbers. Each of us has a social security number, a driver's license number, credit card numbers, military service numbers, telephone numbers and others too numerous to mention. An employee is valued by the number of years of seniority he has, or by the number of clients, sales or products he produces. He values himself by the number he sees on his income tax return on the gross income line. But quantity is not quality, and it never can be.

Elitism and snobbery are narcissistic responses to depersonalization and objectification of the individual. By claiming exclusivity, the elitist or snob is proclaiming himself to be special and unique.

The desire for fortune and fame is intense in our materialistic, technological society, but there is only so much to go around. This breeds dog-eat-dog competition, which reinforces narcissism. Narcissists lack compassion or empathy for others. Winning at the expense of others is no longer popularly regarded as antisocial. The population explosion exacerbates ruthless competition for scarce material resources and for social status.

The world population explosion exacerbates all our social and environmental problems enormously. It took from the beginning of man's time on Earth to 1830, to reach the first billion people. From 1830 to 1930, it doubled, to 2 billion people. It took only 60 years from 1930 to get to 5 billion. In just a few short years, since the year 2000, we've added over a billion more people to the world population, which is projected by experts to double to over 10 billion people within the next 40 years.

The ramifications of the population explosion are severe. Every person needs at least one gallon of fresh water per day. Aquifers are already being depleted. The Great Lakes contain three-fifths of the fresh water on the planet, and lake levels have been dropping for the last decade to new lows. Add to this the serious problem of pollution to the Great Lakes. Underground water is contaminated by toxic wastes, and many wells are drying up due to current demands. Millions of tons of trash and garbage, a mixture of non-biodegradable plastics, toxic chemicals, mercury, lead and methane-producing biodegradables, are discarded daily. It is already a problem finding space for landfills for all this trash, and much of it is dumped into the oceans.

Fisheries are collapsing all around the world. Shallow water fish have all but completely disappeared, due to world demand and subsequent over-harvesting. Deep water fish are now being harvested, for the first time in history, and are in danger of being completely depleted, to the point where they cannot bounce back, within just a few years. The oceans used to be our hope for feeding the huge new population, but that hope is nearly gone, due to short term exploitation. Nations compete for the scarce natural resources that remain. There is little international cooperation on the use of resources that are common to us all. Carbon dioxide and carbon monoxide emissions, along with other fluorocarbons, are destroying the ozone layer that protects us from the harmful rays of the sun, resulting in a 300% increase in deadly skin cancers, and in the 'greenhouse effect'. Global warming of only five degrees will melt the polar ice caps and raise the levels of the oceans enough to completely obliterate coastal nations, such as the Netherlands, states such as Florida, and big cities such as

New York.

The dynamics of supply and demand are going wild, with ever-increasing demand for basic needs met by ever-shrinking supplies. The electric power grid cannot provide the demand for power now, resulting in rolling brown-outs and power outages in California and other Western States and a recent major blackout on the Eastern Seaboard stretching all the way to the Midwest. At the same time, our only source of oxygen is being removed at an alarming rate, to accommodate demands for lumber and land. The tropical rainforests, the source of two-thirds of the oxygen on the planet, are now only one-fifth as large as they once were. How can the world sustain twice as many people as there are now, when resources are already critically scarce?

Geophysical effects are already occurring. Storms are more severe, as are periods of drought. Geological effects are literally erupting all over the globe, exacerbated by the depletion of fossil fuels that took millions and millions of years to form. The hot inner core of the planet is cooling unnaturally, robbed of its fuel. Are we literally killing the living planet? There is no worldwide authority in charge. Instead, nations war over oil and other resources like jackals fighting over a carcass.

At the same time that the world is being polluted and its resources depleted, narcissistic industries utilize precious resources for short-term, materialistic gain. Industries such as cosmetics, jewelry, alcohol and tobacco cater to vanity and addiction. Starvation and AIDS epidemics destroy African nations while conspicuous consumption is practiced in rich industrial nations. Cigarettes are marketed aggressively to the Philippine and Southeast Asian children. Child labor sweat shops produce clothing and shoes that are sold to the oblivious consumers of richer nations.

But people don't want to hear it! Nothing kills a social gathering faster than to mention social inequities and threats to the environment. They'd rather talk about how their investments are doing, or perhaps their new furniture. Narcissists don't care about others, or even their own progeny. They'd rather talk about deep subjects, such as fashion, computers, cars, sports, shoes, television, or movie stars. They care more about what kind of a hair day they're having than about what kind of lives people are living on the other side of the planet, or even down the street. Homeless people wander their own cities, but narcissists avoid the areas where they might have to see one, and when they accidentally do see one, they quickly turn away in disgust. Materialism, apathy and narcissism are in plentiful supply. Supplies of humanistic love, on the contrary, seem to be as scarce as clean water, air and soil.

Our current direction of development has brought us to the brink of ecological and social disaster. We need to overcome our apathy and denial in order to deal with this real global threat. The problems of individuals are a microcosmic reflection of the macrocosm of the world. All of the problems I have explicated for the individual also exist on a worldwide level. We live in a holistic, interconnected world, regardless of whether we recognize it or participate responsibly in it.

The barriers to the development of global consciousness should be obvious. How can one relate lovingly to a stranger from a foreign culture, on the other side of the planet, when one can't even relate to one's neighbors or even to one's own children?

Only through the development of true self love can the cycle of narcissism be defeated and overcome. Individuals must first become constantly aware of their mortality. The awareness of death is powerful, and it inevitably leads us to recognize our priorities. Love is the only priority, when death threatens. People who survive disasters, such as fires, floods, hurricanes, and bombings, suddenly remember that their loved ones are what really matter to them. This is a natural, universal phenomenon. Do we have to wait for disaster before we remember our priorities? Or can we sensitize ourselves to wake up and remember that today is another good day to die, and that each precious day should be Thanksgiving Day and Valentine's Day? An awareness of the reality of death and the life-enhancing power of love is the basis for the development of self-love, which is the opposite of narcissism and the foundation for love of others. Love is the antidote to alienation, depersonalization, desensitization, objectification and materialism. Only the power of love can help us to develop more humanistic attitudes so we can escape from the technological prison.

Can there be such a thing as loving technology? I think there can. If technology is evaluated for its social, moral, environmental and psychological value, rather than merely for its short-term economic value, it can be an instrument of humanistic love. This is not utopian. *It is highly pragmatic and realistic.* If pro-social values are not imposed on technology, then technology may be the end of our species.

Chapter Five

PARENTING FOR THE FUTURE

I have worked with hundreds of children and adolescents for thirty years. Before that, I was one. I have degrees in both psychology and clinical social work. As a professional social worker, I have worked as a group and individual therapist with emotionally impaired and developmentally disabled, and their families, primarily. I've also worked in private practice, with many children whose parents were undergoing divorce. Before becoming a social worker, I was a teacher of creative writing to gifted and talented, on a high school level. Since my semi-retirement from professional social work, my wife (who was also a social worker) and I have been child care providers for pre-schoolers. Both of us have devoted our lives to helping children. I am also a father of three, ranging from 12 to 23 years of age. I have taught parenting skills for many years in a variety of school and agency settings. I have also had some experience as a marital and family therapist.

In my career I have directly observed many phenomenon of child and parental behavior which have led me to the conclusions in this chapter.

I believe that parenting of children is the single most important role that any of us can ever have. As a parent, you not only shape your own children, but you also participate in shaping society. The kind of values you either instill or allow to develop in your children will, collectively, determine the society of the future. Raising children with positive, pro-social values should be everyone's main priority, but it obviously is not, at this point in history.

With more than half of all marriages ending in divorce, children who live with both their natural parents are, for the first time in history, in the minority. The number of children born to single, unmarried mothers is at its highest point in history as well. Father absence, teen suicide, drug and alcohol abuse among minors, and juvenile crime are also at an all time historical high. The severity of juvenile crimes has also increased. There are more murders, rapes and other felonies committed by juveniles today than at any point in our history. Runaway centers are filled to capacity. Homeless teens and children wander the city streets. Obviously, children are alienated. The depersonalizing effects of our materialistic culture have had an enormous negative impact on our children. If we do not make children our priority soon, given the population explosion, these horrendous social problems will multiply exponentially.

The role of parenting is so important to our future as a society that anyone who is a parent should make that role his or her priority, above *all else*, including a career. *No* career is as important as parenting. If we are ever to reverse the current trend of depersonalization, alienation, apathy, materialism and narcissism, then we absolutely must understand and act upon this reality. Parenting a child is the most important thing you will ever do. It is a personal responsibility, and cannot successfully be delegated to another. There is no child who wouldn't benefit from getting more love and attention from a parent, despite how well you think they are doing. Parenting is a social, moral responsibility that supercedes any other role. It is only by recognizing this that we can make the world whole.

It has become commonplace for mothers to arrange for day care for their babies before they are even born. My wife and I experience this phenomena on a regular basis in our child care program.

The trend of placing newborn infants in day care has severe, long term effects on individual children and on society as well. Another popular, destructive misconception that people have about children is that breast feeding is just one of several, equally valuable options. This is a horrible tragedy, perpetrated by a greedy baby formula industry and rationalized by poorly informed, ultimately irresponsible mothers. I am referring to two parent families where the mother chooses her 'career' over the needs of her baby. In the case of single parents, there are other issues. In either case, children and society would both be much better off if mothers of infants did not work and breast-fed their babies.

Breast feeding is not just another option. Children who are breast fed are much healthier, physically, emotionally, and mentally. According to research, breast fed children walk and talk sooner, have fewer illnesses, and attain higher intelligence than formula fed children do. Bottle feeding contributes to chronic ear infections, which can be disastrous for an infant's development. Bottle feeding also impacts negatively on dental development. Beyond the physical and mental benefits of natural breast feeding, there are extremely important emotional benefits. The immense value of intimate mother-child bonding that breast feeding provides cannot be overstated. Breast feeding is the best emotional immunization against narcissism for both the child and the mother that there is. It is the first important interaction of a loving, natural parent with her child. (A planned pregnancy and good prenatal care are the first steps in the process, but breast feeding represents the first actual interaction between mother and child.)

Long term studies have shown that breast fed children develop pro-social behaviors more often and more readily than bottle fed children. They have significantly fewer emotional and social problems and are less likely to be introverted or withdrawn. A mother should breast feed for as long as she can. Every day of breast feeding gives the child an edge in development. To not breast feed is to abandon the child, to at least some degree. Abandonment is the greatest fear of childhood, and damages children emotionally. Ideally, a child who is breast fed will often nurse well into his second year of life, averaging eighteen months to two years.

While breast pumping does provide the physical and mental benefits of breast milk, it does not provide the extremely important mother-child bonding. There are many little 'triggers' in the developing infant brain that are turned on by the wonderful, natural act of breast feeding. Medical researchers are uncovering more of these all the time. No job or career is more important than helping an infant get off to the very best start in life that is possible. The most important and socially valuable role any human can have is to be a good parent. If you can't live up to your responsibility, you shouldn't have children.

If it is a choice between a bigger house and staying home with your pre-school children, be a real mother and tailor your lifestyle to live less expensively, and *be there* for your children and for all of us.

It takes grownups to be good parents. This means having the ability to defer gratification, develop priorities and to plan. If you plan to be a parent, don't buy an expensive house and two cars that will require you both to work. Mothers of pre-school children should never work outside the home unless they absolutely have to. You do not have to be materialistic in your values. What good is it to gain the whole world and sacrifice your child to do it? It's not as if there is a shortage of emotionally damaged people in the world.

As children develop in the first five years, they notice things for the first time, and more every day. They need to be able to share their experiences with their mothers. Child care is not drudgery. It is fascinating and satisfying work of great value to the mother herself, the child and to society.

It is natural for a small child to have his mother nearby, to provide security and safety and to interpret experiences to the child. This is universal in the animal world. One of the most important roles of a parent is to be a teacher. Young children have many teachable moments in a day, and a parent should be there when these windows of learning opportunity open, to guide and shape the child's development. How sad that a child's first words, first steps, first perceptions and interactions happen in day care, where he is one of many, already a number. Objectification and depersonalization start early in children whose mothers abandons them to day care, despite the quality of the day care. Humans are designed to respond better to their own natural parents than to parent substitutes. Research supports this statement. There is not a child alive who would trade a close mother-child bond during his first five years for a more extravagant lifestyle. If you think back to your own early years, you should be able to understand these statements.

At this point, I need to clarify the significant

differences in the mother and father roles. Each parent fills a specific need, and these are distinctly different, though equally important at different points in a child's development.

As a general rule of thumb, during the first nine years of life a child's primary parent is the mother. During the second nine years, from pre-adolescence to young adulthood, the primary parent whom the child needs and relates to is the father. This is because of the primary difference in their roles. The mother is the nurturer, and it is her job to establish a foundation of love. Mothers should provide unconditional love to children. Fathers should also be loving, but their primary role, during the latter nine years of development, is to socialize the child. This is done through conditional responses and role modeling. Research has shown us that these are the primary roles of the two genders in parenting.

The first five years of a child's life are particularly important in the formation of a positive self-concept. The pre-school years are the most intensely needy years that require the most attention from the mother. She is the primary parent for about nine years, to pre-adolescence. Much later, the father's turn for intensive attention comes, during middle adolescence, from 14 through 17. These periods of intensive need are so important that I say, unequivocally, that no mother should work outside the home for the first five years of a child's life, and every father should maximize his time with teens from 14 through 17, even if it means quitting work or going part time while the mother works. Some outside work by the father is preferable, however, because it is part of his role modeling for the adolescents, since his role is to demonstrate how one interacts successfully with the world and in society, as well as setting clear guidelines and limits for the adolescent.

In very general terms, the nurturing of the child is the

main role of the mother, while discipline is the main role of the father. Obviously, both parents should be capable of both roles, but the natural division is as stated. The establishment of a foundation of love is primary, as is the mother's role. As children reach pre-adolescence, at about 9 or 10 years of age, they begin to turn their attention away from the mother and toward the father. Many mothers experience this as a negative loss and feel slighted and treated as servants at this developmental point, but they should realize that it is because they have done their job that it is happening.

As the child enters school, it is also of great value for the mother to be at home when he leaves in the morning and returns in the afternoon. Day care is greatly preferable to a latch-key situation, however. Children and adolescents of all ages need supervision by responsible adults, preferably their own parents.

If children do not separate somewhat from dependency on their mother at this age, it is indicative of immaturity. Growing up is a process of growing away from dependency. In Child Development and Psychology, we call it individuation. The process should occur naturally, and not be rushed. Parents should not expect children to be or act older than what is appropriate for their chronological age. On the other hand, behavior such as age-inappropriate baby talk, biting, clinging or bed wetting are significant signals from the child of immaturity and regression and should be taken very seriously.

The father is the predominant parent during the second nine years of development because his responses are conditional. He represents society to a child, and it is his job to socialize the child, now that the child's brain development has progressed to the level of abstract thought.

Research in child development has shown that

socialization of the child comes almost exclusively from the father. This includes gender identity, for both boys and girls. This means that the father must be assertive and definite to be effective. Patience and humor are two valuable tools for any active father. Fathers who listen four parts to every one part of talk are the most effective. It is better to be firm, not stern. It is of utmost importance to be consistent in discipline. When a father has his job on his mind, it is difficult to concentrate on discipline and role modeling for children. A good father *orchestrates* positive learning experiences for his children.

Studies on father absence have shown that absent or passive fathers produce both severe depression and aggression in both boys and girls.Children with absent fathers have significantly higher incidents of suicide and drug abuse.

What is not at an all time high is parental time spent with children. Quite the contrary is the norm. A recent study concluded that fathers average less than 10 minutes a day with their children. Mothers who work out of the home often leave their children in day care for eleven hours a day. Subtracting sleeping time, which for smaller children should be nine or ten hours per night, and various homemaking tasks, such as meal preparation and house cleaning, children do not get anywhere near the amount of time they need with either parent.

There is no such thing as "quality time" where children are concerned. Too often, parents use the excuse that they spend "quality time", as opposed to a quantity of time, with their children. This is defined as doing something "special" together, such as a treat of some kind. Often this means passive entertainment, like a movie or a sports event, where parent-child interaction is at a minimum. Regardless of the nature of the "quality time", the effect is that of a feast

or famine of time spent with the child. Many adults today have great difficulty in spending time with their children. They feel uncomfortable and provide only mere presence, as the children play in a park or watch television. What children actually love, and desperately need, is loving *interaction* with their parents. And, they need really a lot of it, much more than parents generally realize. Children go through their developmental changes quickly, and parents need to be there, physically, to share and help shape these myriad and constant changes.

Children are categorically different from adults in numerous ways. For one thing, they *think* differently.

The French developmental and experimental psychologist Jean Piaget proved that children do not begin to think many abstract thoughts much before the age of eight. Moral choices between right and wrong are based in an individual's ability to think abstractly. Adults persist in making abstract moral statements to children despite the fact that children cannot comprehend these kinds of ideas. Children learn through repetition and consequences before the age of eight, unless the child is exceptional. This kind of learning requires time for repetition and for providing consequences. Parents often react with horror when small children steal, lie, or commit other amoral acts, instead of patiently teaching the child through repetition and consequence. "Don't you *know* that stealing is *wrong*?" They ask, outraged. Of course, children do not know how to choose between right and wrong - these are abstractions. Children do not think like adults.

On the other hand, adults often think that children *feel* differently than adults, another major misconception. Children have sensitive feelings that are similar to those of an adult in most ways. When they are ignored or dismissed as "just children", their feelings are hurt. Children need a great deal of affection from significant others in order to feel loved and unique. Adults are often shy to give open affection to children, especially as they reach adolescence, when, ironically, they need it intensely.

Children are dependent on adults and will prefer even negative attention to none at all, unlike a mature adult. The greatest fear of childhood is abandonment by parents. Children who experience abandonment act out in anger or inwardly with sadness and self-destructive behaviors. I have worked closely with numerous abandoned and abused children. Most would readily choose continued abuse if only they could continue to live with the parents who abused them.

Many of these children 'set themselves up' for rejection by others, because they have lost the will to hope for acceptance and feel more in control when they actually cause the rejection, which they have come to feel is inevitable. These children are deeply damaged in their ability to trust and bond with others, often for the rest of their lives.

I am always amazed at how much credence adults put in talking to children. Children rarely, if ever, learn from listening to adults talk. Children learn best from *demonstration*. It is far better, and more convincing, to demonstrate affection to a child than to say "I love you.". Love is an abstraction, a word. Affection and attentive listening to a child demonstrate love in a concrete and tangible way. Children need to have love *demonstrated* to them every day, several times a day, in order for them to form the foundation of a healthy self-concept. This requires lots of time and devotion on the part of parents and other significant adults. Again, there simply is no substitute. No child will ever "do what you say, not what you do". They are not built that way.

Although children are not great listeners, they are astute observers. Psychologist Albert Bandura has demonstrated that children learn largely through vicarious observation. Bandura's long term studies proved that children learn more readily through observation, called vicarious learning, than through behavioral reinforcement. Children are natural mimics. Lower primates, such as chimpanzees, also are adept at mimicking actions they have only observed. Children who see affectionate displays between their parents are both happier and more affectionate themselves than children who do not see such demonstrations of affection. Conversely, children who see (vicariously experience) violence are themselves more likely to act violently. Allowing children to see violent imagery in movies or on television is one of the primary causes of increased violence among juveniles. Adults may understand, for example, that professional wrestling is staged entertainment, but young pre-adolescent children truly do not understand this, despite what they may parrot back to the indulgent, irresponsible parent who lets them watch it. Talk, including their own, means little to a child. Action means much more. If it looks real to a child, then it is. If it looks manly, then that's what men do. If a boy wants to be a man, and the imagery he has seen repeatedly of men is one of violence, then he begins to mimic the behavior, so he can be a man too.

If you want your son to be a sensitive man, model it for him, and restrict his exposure to negative imagery. If you want your daughter to be more than a sexual object, restrict her exposure to that kind of imagery and model the positive kind. Albert Bandura developed the concept of positive role-modeling for children. His writings are valuable reading for all serious parents.

Children are insecure in their parents' love. They are dependent on parents, and regardless of how they present themselves, need large amounts of affection and attention to build a good self-concept. Only the most secure children or adolescents will openly ask for more attention and time with their parents. The others will signal their needs through attention seeking behaviors as widely diverse as aggression and severe withdrawal. I have been amazed, working with children for over thirty years, at how responsive they are when their basic need for attention and affection has been met. I have seen kids who were severely traumatized and abused bounce back when an adult showed interest in them. One of the first realizations I had, when I first started working with abused children, was that children are remarkably resilient, once their unmet needs are met. They are not small adults. They are dependent, insecure persons who need many demonstrations that they are valued and worthy of time and attention.

Children feel more secure when they know where they stand. Youngsters are fascinated by rules. That is why games are so significant to children age 5 through 12. Behavioral limits strengthen a child's development of all important ego-boundaries. Parents should be assertive in their shaping of a child's behavior and the subsequent values that are learned through discipline.

Discipline is not a bad thing. Discipline is not the same as punishment. The word 'discipline' comes from the same root word as the word 'disciple', which means 'a learner'. Punishment, on the other hand, means 'to hurt'. Children should never be punished, but they should always be disciplined. Discipline and nurturing are two sides of the same coin. A child who is not disciplined will not develop self-discipline, nor will he feel loved. By providing discipline to a child, you are demonstrating that you care about him. Children know this.

Physical punishment should never be used except as a truly last resort, and then only when the child himself has demonstrated violence to another. The discipline should fit the 'crime', in order for it to be a good learning experience. This requires some thought and creativity on the part of the parent or adult. If children are your priority, you will be quite able to develop creative discipline.

Children who regress or become arrested in skills are in some kind of trouble. It could be emotional or even developmental, and a professional should be consulted when such behaviors persist. A pediatrician, child psychologist or a children's social worker are three types of professionals who can help under this circumstance.

Parents should be equally concerned with a child's mental and emotional health as they are with his physical health.

Subtle hostile behaviors should be quickly identified and responded to. When behaviors are subtle, such as complaining, whining, pouting, sarcasm, verbal aggression or negative facial expressions, giving a verbal response is usually enough. This 'nips' more aggressive behaviors 'in the bud'. The child or adolescent feels that his parent is attentive to him and cares enough to give him guidance before he loses control. When this is done consistently, you'll never have to deal with more upsetting, serious behaviors. Children should be shaped from infancy in this way. My wife and I are often amazed at the ineffectiveness and non-assertiveness of parents, when they report that their small child "wouldn't go to bed until eleven", or "wouldn't let me change him". These must be awfully powerful children! Children who become little dictators in their homes will have severe adjustment problems in school and perhaps society. They become narcissistic and develop an exaggerated concept of their own importance.

It is even more important and effective to 'catch them being good'. Studies of behavioral reinforcement have shown that positive reinforcement is the most effective of all, much more effective than negative. Negative consequences should relate to the negative behavior of the child. For example, if a child breaks something due to carelessness or intentionally, he should do some kind of work to help pay for its replacement. Taking away television, or sending him to his room, although negative contingencies, are not related to the specific misbehavior, so are not as effective as a learning experience that helps the child make greater sense of the way the world works.

Positive reinforcement can be verbal, accompanied by a smile or an affectionate hug. Some parents are so shy when responding to children's behaviors that they would benefit from actually counting the number of times they gave a response, both positive and negative. Time spent with an adult, such as playing ball, going to a park, reading together,singing or drawing together, is the best way to give a child positive reinforcement. Also, children respond to good humor and to smiles. They love to be joked with and to act silly with a parent, and I heartily recommend it. I am known as a funny Daddy myself.

When it comes to toys, it is best to avoid electronic or technical toys that essentially play with themselves for the child. A child learns more and develops more with toys he can manipulate. There are four main categories of toys which provide growth opportunities for children: 1) Athletic toys, such as balls, bicycles or tricycles, pogo sticks, sleds, skates, darts, water toys, etc.; 2) Artistic toys, such as painting and drawing materials, musical instruments and toys, clay and costumes; 3) Building toys, such as Lincoln Logs, Waffle blocks, Legos, wooden blocks, erector sets, etc.; 4) Animal toys, such as stuffed plush animals, plastic animal figures, dinosaurs, etc. All of these kinds of toys encourage self-expression, creativity and development of skills. In addition, children benefit enormously from books and reading together. Frequent use of the Public Library is highly recommended. Books stimulate children's imaginations and mental development. In my own childhood, some of my happiest moments were when my mother would sit and read poetry to my sister and me.

Children should also be introduced and exposed to nature as much as possible. Wildlife sanctuaries and parks should be used regularly to help connect children to the natural world and teach them how to relax. Teach your children that they are not the center of the universe but are an important part of it. Show them the enormity and complexity of nature.

Sibling relationships are extremely important and should be strongly encouraged and orchestrated. Children under the age of 10 benefit from rooming together, regardless of gender. Bunk beds are perfectly suited for this purpose. Separate rooms at this age are not necessarily a good thing, as they encourage isolation. Your goal as a parent is to instill values such as sharing and reciprocity, and rooming younger children together is an excellent way to further these pro-social goals. A close sibling relationship that continues past the elementary years can be one of the best antidotes to negative peer influence during adolescence. Frequent contacts with grandparents and other relatives also develop family bonding and identification. These contacts can prevent family isolation and may, to some degree, help keep an adolescent from becoming overly identified with peers. Do you want your children to be close to each other as adults? Rooming them together increases the likelihood of good adult friendships between them. They will have more shared experiences and mutual memories, be less selfish, and feel less lonely and more secure.

When, at adolescence or shortly before, a child finally does get his own room, he will value it more, and it can be a rite of passage that signifies his individuation and maturation specifically at the time it is appropriate. While you don't want to grant adult privileges to adolescents, greater freedoms and choices that are *age appropriate* should be granted in little increments. The child will be pleased that he is making progress *toward* adulthood, but at the same time secure and safe that he does not have to make adult choices prematurely. Increasing allowance *gradually*, awarding *gradually* later bedtimes, assigning *gradually* more complex household tasks and responsibilities, help the child ease into adolescence and finally adulthood. Some children can move faster and further than others. Be as realistic as you can, because their futures depend on it.

Eating regularly with the family is also highly beneficial and should be a priority. I am a great believer in the value of dinner music. In my family, we always play some music on the stereo while we eat together.

I also think that use of babysitters should be minimal. If you have time for recreation, why not include your children? Anything you can do to maximize family togetherness is of great value. A family game night is an excellent idea. Doing things together helps the child to identify with the parents and their values.

Special outings enhance family bonding and the personal growth of children. Museums, botanical gardens,

Art museums and galleries, zoos, plays at Civic Theaters, musical concerts, the circus, county fairs, visiting different parks and libraries, parades, beaches, boating, skating, hiking, nature centers, etc. all provide great shared memories and expansion of the child's experiential base. Taking a child to a restaurant helps him to understand how to behave in public and use good manners.

In addition to whole family outings, special outings between one parent and one child are special indeed. My youngest son loves to go fishing with me. My daughter and I go on 'dates'. Every year we go to a Daddy-Daughter Valentine dance together. It is a special tradition between the two of us that we both look forward to. My sons have accompanied me when I needed to fix something around the house, go to the hardware store, lumber store, etc. My wife and daughter love to garden together.

Another way to enhance family bonding is with a family pet. Both dogs and cats are ideal for this purpose. Children love pets and can also help care for them. More exotic pets don't work as well as dogs and cats. With a dog, there is the additional benefit of walks and playing active games. A dog can bring a lot of joy to a family, well worth the effort it takes to maintain him.

All of this may seem rather obvious, but in the light of eroding traditional family values, I would rather take the chance of preaching to the converted than let issues go unmentioned. Consistently doing the average thing can take quite a lot of effort for parents, and sometimes they forget, with so many options bombarding them.

To we who work in child mental health, a type of anti-social personality disorder has emerged in the last quarter century that is marked by a lack of conscience and severe rage. Not only are these juveniles without conscience, but they are often pathologically angry and sadistic toward others. The number of these severe anti-social teens, both boys and girls, increases every year. This has been the universal observation of social workers and psychologists who specialize in working with adolescents. Caseloads of juvenile probation officers are at an all time high. The apathetic prefer to ignore these patterns, being preoccupied with their own narcissistic concerns.

The anti-social teens are severely alienated. But, being adolescents, they are peer-oriented. As a result, a teen culture with shared anti-social values has developed. Anti-social social groups in the form of juvenile gangs, are at an all time high.

Adolescents love to talk, but talking to them has many of the same limitations as talking to children. Adolescents enjoy being listened *to*, and are often surprised when an adult is patient enough to do so. When I was a therapist in a home for emotionally impaired children, I was assigned a boy of 15 who had a long history of severe temper tantrums. The county worker who placed him at our facility expressed doubt that we could handle his behavior, as he was a very large, heavy boy with a short fuse whose tantrums were frequent and legendary. The first time I saw him for therapy, I didn't speak much. I concentrated instead on making good eye contact with him and smiling. It took most of the hour for him to look relaxed. When he did, I smiled and asked if he felt a little better. He nodded, and that was the session. I instructed the workers in the house to call me if he was balking at instructions or showing any sign of stress. When this happened, they'd ask if he wanted to see me, and he'd say he did. After a week or two, he began to relax as soon as he saw me, and he slowly began to talk to me about how frustrated he felt. His parents were in their sixties, and he was the only child left at home. All his siblings were much older than he and had families of their own. His parents were quiet people who had been farmers. The boy had experienced an isolated childhood with no one to talk to. When he was old enough for school, he was socially inept and felt nervous and isolated. By the time he was fifteen, he had developed the pattern of blowing up when frustrated, and this cemented his isolation from others but ended their making fun of him, as they were then frightened of him. He loved his parents, but doubted that they loved him. They never talked to each other, much, or to him.

After six months, during which I listened to him four parts to one part talking, he started visiting his parents on weekends. Remarkably, he had only had two tantrums at our facility during that whole time, though he had therapy almost every day.

After the first three or four weekend visits with his parents, he was becoming agitated again. He said that things were no different at home. They still didn't talk to him, much, although I'd visited them and emphasized the importance of taking to the boy, to draw him out and connect with him. They were simply old and tired, but I could see that they were good people who loved their son but felt overwhelmed by him.

So, after a few of these visits, I asked the boy why he didn't take the lead and talk to his parents, to draw *them* out? He looked very frustrated, and said "I just can't talk to adults!" I replied that he talked to me all the time. He looked at me as if I were daft. "But, you're not a real adult!" he said. This was one of the nicest compliments a client ever gave me. Sadly, however, he had formed a generalized image of adults as untrustworthy and uninterested in what he had to say. After six more months, during which I switched to family sessions every week, he finally went back home. His parents eventually did become more demonstrative, though it took some work. The rest of his adolescence was tantrum free and he finished high school.

Most adolescents are incapable of self-supervision. Adolescents are even more given to peer mimicry and vicarious learning than younger children, even though they do have some ability to think abstractly. This is due to their emotional intensity, fueled by hormones. Their thinking is underdeveloped and primitive and their focus is on peers. They tend to be highly critical of adult beliefs and attitudes, as they are exercising their new found ability to think critically. This makes adolescents high risk for making serious mistakes in social and personal judgement. Adolescents need supervision, all the time. It is when they are unsupervised that they get into trouble. Lack of supervision also affects the adolescent's fragile self-concept. Even the cockiest adolescent is deeply unsure of himself and experiencing a developmental identity crisis. Adolescence is a transitional period between childhood and adulthood. As such, it is an unstable and confusing period of life.

Because adolescents seek independence, often adults give in to their demands, and let them go unsupervised when they really shouldn't. Unsupervised children are not safe, nor do they feel secure. Unsupervised time is when they make often life-altering mistakes. A child or adolescent should never be unsupervised in their television or video viewing, nor in their use of the internet. Parents need to interpret experiences to adolescents as much as possible. Adolescents need responses on almost everything they say and do.

Once I was conducting a group therapy session with some adolescent boys. The exchange went like this: a boy asked another what time he had to be in the house at night.

The other boy, a satisfied look on his face, replied " I have to be in before dark. What time do you have to be in?" The other boy looked sad as he replied, in a hurt voice, "Oh...I can come in whenever I want." Everyone in that group understood that the boy who had to come in before dark felt more loved than the boy who didn't.

Adolescents want to know that adults care enough about them to keep them safe, even from themselves. I have seen numerous illustrations of this in my work as a therapist.

Adolescents have a need for external structure in their lives. Their ego-boundaries are fuzzy and externally imposed rules and guidelines help them to feel secure. Adults often give adolescents too many choices, out of a basic misunderstanding of the differences between adolescents and adults. Adolescents feel more secure when adults are *definitive*.

A regular bedtime is important for all ages, including adolescents. It is a popular misconception that teenagers should be allowed to choose their own bedtimes and to come and go as they please. Too much freedom, too soon, can have disastrous results. Think twice before you let a teen own a car, work outside the home or date. Childhood is so short. Seventeen is when the above activities should be considered. Prior to that is likely to lead to life-altering mistakes. This is not a matter of trust. It is a matter of judgement and parental responsibility. Delaying adult freedoms won't hurt an adolescent, although it may irritate him. Too much, too soon can kill or maim him, however. Remember when in doubt, the answer should be 'no'.

I understand that my comments may not have popular appeal to those who want to rationalize their lifestyles. I do not seek popularity, but the truth. There is too much at stake.

Spending time with children enhances quality of life

immeasurably. I have spent nearly every day of my adult life interacting with children, and it has helped me to feel young, involved and happy. When the children have been abused, disturbed or disabled, I have done my best to help them in whatever way I could, and this has given tremendous meaning to my life. *There is no better way to help society than to help children.* I would not trade the inner riches I've gained from helping children, and learned from them, for all the materialistic riches in the world. I can say this truthfully, and my conscience is clear. How's yours?

Everyone doesn't have to become a professional social worker or teacher. If you will just make your own children your priority, and recognize how extremely important the job of parenting is, and put aside materialistic concerns in favor of being much more active as a parent,you will be doing your part in building a better world for everybody. The truth of this is self-evident. Children need you, and we all need them.

Chapter Six

Whole Self

The connection between materialism and narcissism and the symptoms of apathy, depersonalization and alienation have both social and individual manifestations. In this chapter I will focus on the correlation between beliefs, attitudes and feelings, less on the social effects and more on the effects on the individual. I will examine the phenomena of fundamental, core beliefs, and how they lead to certain specific feelings.

Our perception of reality is based on our beliefs. Experience is *interpreted* by reference to our belief systems. We see what we have trained ourselves to see, and feel accordingly. If too many of us are narcissistic, apathetic and alienated, it is because our belief systems are flawed and dysfunctional. If we have created a depersonalizing society, instead of a world that is equitable to all, it is because our social structures and institutions reflect a fundamentally materialistic and narcissistic system of beliefs. It is time we examined these more closely.

Fundamental Core Beliefs

Everyone has a philosophy of life. While it may be largely subconscious, each person has a belief system, which addresses two fundamental philosophical questions which form the foundation for attitudes and perception, and which in turn are manifested in emotions. These philosophical questions and the positions which are fundamental to a belief system, are 1) Free will versus determinism (fate), and 2) The moral nature of man (inherently good, bad or neutral?).

Attitudes are secondary to basic beliefs. Most people are consciously aware of their attitudes, but awareness of the fundamental core beliefs upon which their attitudes are based, is much less common. There is a direct linkage between basic beliefs and feelings, yet few people examine their beliefs when their emotions are disturbed. Indeed, it is difficult for people to do this, because their basic core beliefs have been subjectively ratified by experience. Beliefs alter perception and interpretation of events in a self-affirming way. In other words, we tend to see what we want to see, regardless of how it makes us feel.

One core philosophical issue that each person takes a belief-position on is free will versus fate or predetermination. If one believes that he has no free will, he does not, in effect, have it, because he doesn't attempt to exercise it. If one does believe in free will, despite whatever is objectively true, he will have a wider range of choice, and his experiences, in turn, will tend to confirm his basic belief.

Free will is essential to an ability to love, as Rollo May pointed out in his book *Love and Will*. Loving is a pro-active choice. One determines that he loves a specific person, and that no one else will do. Love is not based on the materialistic value of the love object, but rather, on his intrinsic and unique internal qualities.

94

Sometimes the external circumstances of lovers seem incompatible, from the view of others, because the lovers are responding to each other's inner selves. The classic illustration of this phenomena is Shakespeare's *Romeo and Juliet*. The right to exercise free will in the area of love is universal in Western culture. How many people have left the Catholic Church because they chose to love and marry a non-Catholic, despite the rule that all Catholics must marry within the Church? Their choice of whom to love reflects a belief in free will, despite strong, consistent efforts to influence them to the contrary.

The other, related, philosophical issue which takes on the status of a core belief is the question of the moral nature of man. Is man inherently good, bad, or neutral in his very nature? This core belief-choice is related to the degree of optimism, pessimism or neutrality that forms a person's expectations from society and fellow men in general.

If a person believes that man is essentially good by nature, he will have a hard time reconciling his belief with the greedy and evil deeds that men do. Of course, he will rationalize these concerns in order to confirm his pre-existent belief. Putting it together with a belief in determinism, he will say that circumstances led born-good people to do selfish and evil things. So too, will a person who believes that people are essentially born-bad, rationalize evil human deeds to confirm his bias. He will have a more difficult time explaining the selfless and altruistic deeds of very good people.

Both of these positions on the nature of man are essentially deterministic. A person who believes in free will will tend to think that the world is made up of both kinds of people, and that man's nature is morally neutral. His expectations of others are less likely to disappoint or amaze him. He develops a realistic understanding of others and of himself. He learns that he has to continuously make choices between moral alternatives. He develops an active, internal moral code to which he can refer. A belief that man is morally neutral and needs to choose between good and bad results in more realistic expectations towards others and toward oneself. It is the foundation of a strong sense of self (ego).

How our basic core beliefs interact largely determines how expansive our ego-boundaries can be. Ironically, and paradoxically, a schizophrenic may have, in one sense, overly expansive ego-boundaries, so that he cannot tell where he ends and others begin. But that state, of severe mental illness, can also be conceptualized as an *impacted* ego-boundary, that is so small that there is little or no sense of self.

Extremely altruistic persons are often seen as having expansive ego-boundaries. They are said to be *at one with the world*. This phenomena is generally recognized by all the major world religions as a high state of spirituality. From a social point of view, we can probably at least agree that it would be a better world if societies and cultures, otherwise known as people, were less divided and more *identified* with each other. United, we may stand, while divided we fall.

Locus of Control

A person's *locus of control* is a major attitudinal component of his intellectual and emotional functioning. *Locus of control* refers to whether a person thinks that his thoughts, feelings and actions are more controlled by internal or external factors. It is consistent for a person who has an internalized locus of control to believe in free will. One needs to believe in free will in order to exercise it. In principle, components of a person's belief system are consistent from one level of abstraction to another. Thus, whole sets of beliefs, attitudes, behaviors and feelings are generally consistent and interrelated.

A person who has a core belief in fate will naturally develop an external locus of control. Such a person will take less responsibility for his choices in life, feeling that he is a victim of circumstance and a leaf blown about by the winds of fate. An external locus of control causes a person to be reactive, rather than proactive, in dealing with life situations. When things go badly, he often feels overwhelmed and resourceless. Conversely, when things go well, his self-concept is not positively reinforced to the same degree as that of an internally controlled person.

An internal locus of control stimulates personal growth, because when bad things happen, the person takes responsibility and learns from it, and when good things happen, the person accepts credit for his part in it. If one blames external forces for outcomes of situations where he might have made a better, more pro-active choice, the only thing that is reinforced is the belief that he is largely controlled by external circumstances.

It is not difficult to guess which type of person is happier. An external locus of control most usually results in roller coaster emotions - happy when circumstances go well, sad or angry when they don't. An internalized locus of control results in a more stabile coping style, not so determined by events. Such a person develops stronger ego-boundaries and better personality integration.

If you want to inculcate a sense of personal responsibility in a child, and thus improve the world, teach him to maintain an internal locus of control. In my many years of work with emotionally disturbed children, I came to recognize that an externalized locus of control was a basic symptom of emotional disturbance. When a disturbed child is confronted for a misbehavior, he invariably blames circumstances or his accomplice. "He *made* me do it!" is the oft repeated phrase. Disturbed adults blame society for their crimes. Hitler's generals were 'only following orders'.

Compelled by external circumstances, we become automatons with no personal responsibility for our choices. A man may become a leaf in the wind, if he surrenders his free will and responsibility.

Erich Fromm, in his book *Escape From Freedom*, asserts that most people are more comfortable as slaves and automatons than they are as free individuals who have to make choices.

Because the internally oriented person is more pro-active than the externally oriented person, he, paradoxically, may also care more about the future of mankind. He may, pro-actively, work for the future, because his ego-boundaries have expanded to include the welfare of others. In other words, his identity is secure enough that he expands it to identify with others. A core belief in free will has as its end result a more socially positive world.

Thinking Style

A belief in free will is also related to a person's thinking style. A person who is capable of divergent thinking as opposed to convergent thinking, is more flexible, creative and adaptable. Divergent thinking is the ability to consider an issue from different, seemingly opposite angles. Convergent thinking is rigid and fixated on one particular interpretation of a situation or an issue.

Materialistic thinking is highly convergent. When a materialist fixates on a desired object, such as a certain item of furniture, for example, he will hunt for that particular item until he finds it. If it is unavailable, he will continue to yearn for it anyway. He's always wanted one of those! He'll never give up until he has one. His happiness depends on it.

A divergent thinker, on the other hand, is flexible. He questions his own desires and choices, and considers alternatives. If the item he originally chooses is unavailable, he moves on. He accepts an alternative, or even, as the Zen Buddhists do, surrenders his desire altogether for the thing. His divergent thinking allows him to achieve resolution. He considers not doing or having something equally to doing or having something. Divergent thinking is more creative and flexible than convergent thinking. It is the large, stiff trees that blow over in a high wind, not the little, flexible ones.

A divergent thinker is able to adapt himself to ever changing circumstances and is more likely to rise to a situational challenge than a convergent thinker. A person who believes in fate will tend to be externally locused, believe that man is either by nature good or bad, and a convergent thinker. Such a person often feels overwhelmed by life and emotionally tends toward disturbances such as chronic anger, depression, apathy and helplessness.

Blind acceptance of a new technology, such as personal computers, is an example of convergent thinking. Convergent thinkers tend to be conformists that jump on whatever bandwagon that passes by. They would not take it upon themselves to question the judgement of the majority, much like the lemmings, who confidently follow each other into the sea, or the Germans under Adolf Hitler.

A divergent thinker is more likely to look for the negative side effects of a technology. He may not be willing to trade off his privacy or his human processes for a personal computer. He may think that his children will be better off without immediate gratification in their research, preferring the more difficult, but ultimately more valuable process of using actual books for research. Ironically, he will be viewed as a 'have not' by his computer-owning neighbors, while he considers that what he has not is computer crime, time-consuming trivial emails, loss of privacy, depersonalization and the devotion of space in his home to another machine. Information inflation devalues information. Removing the human from the thinking process renders it emotionally cold and uncreative. Instant gratification lowers one's attention span and concurrently causes dependency. If a divergent thinker decides that a personal computer is right for him, after considering the pros and cons, his choice will, at least, be an informed decision. The ability to think divergently increases self-sufficiency and promotes independence.

A divergent thinker probably believes in free will, thinks that man is morally neutral, and maintains a more homeostatic emotional state.

Feeling Styles

Good mental hygiene can be attained through consideration and adjustment of one's basic belief system. One system is simply less functional than the other. The formula which has been adopted by twelve-step programs such as Alcoholics Anonymous, is based on the relationship between action, acceptance, courage and wisdom. A similar principle may be found in Buddhism and other world religions. Serenity is said to come from having the courage to change that which can be changed, the ability to accept that which cannot be changed, and the wisdom to know the difference between them. Inner peace comes to those who are flexible and who can think divergently, discriminating between things that can and cannot be changed. Courage is the emotional component. Courage and choice are inextricably connected.

On the list of things you cannot change, death is number one. In the stages of grieving, acceptance is the final stage. A person who has oriented himself to the everyday reality of potential death has put life in perspective and is likely to find that acceptance of smaller inconveniences is relatively easy. He develops a realistic attitude that things could always be worse and does not experience the self-imposed emotional stress of a less adaptable person. Traumatic events, such as a house fire, a sudden accident that threatens the life or health of a loved one, or a physical battle demand that a person be at his best form, to make quick decisions that may determine the final outcome of the event. Immediate acceptance of the reality of the situation may often be the difference between disaster and survival.

Anger is the result of convergent thinking. Anger is a denial of reality, an inflexible resistance to the acceptance of something that has already occurred. It is a waste of energy. It really is better to light one candle than to curse the darkness. A convergent thinker who lacks the wisdom to know the difference between things that can and cannot be changed, will not adapt to circumstances with a constructive response. He will get mad, kick the car that won't start, rail at the unfairness of things, and in short, curse the darkness ineffectually.

Anger is always a reaction to some reality that we don't want to accept. It is the opposite of acceptance. It is reactive. Those whose locus of control is external often experience anger, or may even live in a constant state of anger. Physiologically, one minute of anger alters the blood chemistry for approximately thirteen hours. The physiological component of anger stresses the body enormously, and has been confirmed by medical research. If

101

a person is prone to anger, and gets angry in the morning, and again in the evening, it is like taking an anger-pill, because his blood chemistry would *always* contain the toxic hormonal chemicals that are released through anger. On the other hand, smiling, laughing and loving produce brain chemicals that can prevent disease and strengthen the body's immune system, called endorphins. Beliefs and attitudes ultimately impact on both emotional and physical health.

The dynamic of depression is generally defined by mental health professionals as 'anger turned against the self'. Depression is characterized by immobilization, withdrawal, and pessimism. Persons who are chronically depressed have an external locus of control, and a convergent thinking style. Clinical depression occurs when the blood chemistry is chronically low in endorphins and high in the toxins produced by anger. Thus, there are both mental and physical conditions that are associated with depression.

The physical symptoms in depression are secondary to the emotional, in most cases, although brain dysfunction can also be the cause of depression, in which case the emotional symptoms are secondary, though just as real. In such cases, medication is most helpful, but the chronically depressed person must also learn to interpret events differently, take positive action, and think more effectively.

Pessimism is an attitude of negativity and hopelessness. It is directly based in convergent thinking, because hopelessness is the inability to see positive options. The immobilization of the depressive person is also a manifestation of convergent thinking. He is unable to interpret external events in a flexible and divergent manner. He is fixated and lacks the internal resources to take meaningful and positive action. He believes in fate, and this belief produces hopelessness.

In treatment, we try to first get a depressed person to express himself, as depression is a case of severe withdrawal. The ego-boundaries are impacted and shrunken in depression. Although depressives tend to have an externalized locus of control, they are often also severely introspective, which they cannot handle, given their convergent thinking style. To counter the immobilization, a depressed person needs to get in touch with his anger and redirect it externally.

When a person with an external locus of control and a convergent thinking style is overwhelmed by external events, and reactively internalizes, he does not have the self discipline of a divergent thinker who has attained a level of comfort with an internal locus of control. He finds himself on very shaky, unfamiliar territory. Although his anger is unrealistic, as all anger is, it is a relatively healthier response to an overwhelming situation than depression and withdrawal. Anger can be worked with, by developing acceptance and action steps, whereas depression is a psychologically immobile state where the ego-boundaries are pulled- in and at least temporarily 'stuck' there.

All negative feelings are essentially variations or combinations of anger and depression. Alienation is often a combination of the two. The *Serenity Prayer* alluded to previously is really a formula for resolving bad feelings. One must learn to differentiate between things that can be changed and things that must be accepted. Convergent thinking is the antitheses of serenity. Divergent thinking is the key to adaptability and coping. An externalized locus of control is ultimately incompatible with a divergent thinking style. A belief in fate is fatal to good mental health.

The goal of psychotherapy is to help a person become more responsible for his thoughts, feelings and actions. It is helpful to conceptualize responsibility by breaking it into two words: response ability. A belief in man's neutral moral nature leads to acceptance of responsibility, because one has to choose between good and evil continuously. The legal standard for sanity used by the courts is the ability to recognize the difference between right and wrong. Thus, an internal moral code is the universal basis for the social contract.

The function of the ego is to mediate between the internal needs and desires of the person and the external world. One can only interact successfully with the world when reality is accepted. Acceptance of reality is the major problem of humanity. Appropriate social change and progress is dependent on the development of the individuals that make up society. Individuals need to assess their belief systems, including a recognition of their locus of control, thinking styles, feeling styles, orientation to time and personal responsibility.

Time Competency

Another factor in good mental hygiene is an individual's competency with time. Time competency refers to the ability of a person to stay centered in the here-and-now. Anxiety results when a person's thoughts dwell on stressful rehashing of negative events that are already in the past. The past is something that cannot be changed. Anxiety also results when a person dreads future events or mentally rehearses how he will respond to an anticipated event. The present is forgotten, and the person is inattentive to what is happening around him. The inability to focus on the here-and-now is a distinct handicap that prevents a person from giving his best to his performance in the present.

Time incompetency is also dysfunctional because it prevents relaxation, which is an important element in the enjoyment of life. Quality of life is greatly enhanced by an ability to relax. It is an important principle in Buddhism that one needs to empty his mind of thoughts in order to experience nature and relax the ego, letting go of trivial desires and experiencing life more directly. Transcendental meditation is based on this principle and has been shown through clinical research to significantly reduce both emotional and physical stress.

A constant awareness of death encourages greater time competency. To dwell on the past or the future is to forfeit the present. Gestalt psychology has demonstrated that one can only focus on one thought at any given moment. Present time is real, and all we ever really have. The past is gone, and the future is just a fantasy. Memory is highly subjective and selective. Two people share the same real moment, but each will remember it differently, because of individual perceptual differences.

The past, like death, is something that cannot be changed. Time spent wandering through memories destroys future memories of the present, which becomes the past. Paying attention to the present, while suspending attitudinal judgement as best we can, makes these the 'good old days'. Similarly, to live for the future is to sacrifice the present for the sake of a fantasy.

Another aspect of time competency is addressed in the book *Type A Behavior and Your Heart,* by Meyer Friedman. People with type-A behavior are driven by time constraints and feel them as intense pressure to perform. They cannot relax, and as a result their bodies deteriorate rapidly from all the stress. They have an external locus of control.

Good mental hygiene is basically a combination of self-discipline and self-awareness. A person needs to be aware of his fundamental core beliefs and how they determine his attitudes, locus of control, thinking and feeling styles and his ability to appreciate and deal with the present. Your basic beliefs may need reevaluation. An internal locus of control, a divergent thinking style and time competency are keys to good mental hygiene and high quality of life.

Chapter Seven

Whole World

Respectable scientists, such as the late Carl Sagan, have informed us that the universe is so immense that it is absolutely inconceivable that we are the only so-called 'intelligent life' in it. While many may feel that the astronomer's proclamation that aliens exist is radical, it is actually highly conservative. They are probably being diplomatic in consideration of how short-sighted and primitive they consider their audience to be, many of whom are convinced that the creation mythology of their particular religion is, in fact, undisputable, objective truth. Despite ample evidence, many people continue to reject evolutionism. A few even continue to believe in the Tooth Fairy and The Easter Bunny. Satanists believe in the Devil, and scare the hell out of others who believe in the Devil too, but don't like him.

Privately, I am sure that these politically sensitive and diplomatic scientists understand that not only is the universe so big that intelligent alien life must exist, but that it is so big that anything we can conceive of, with our limited imaginations and time, must be true and real *somewhere*. If this 'blows your mind', be glad. Your mind needs to be shaken out of its complacency.

There are billions of stars, and each, in its stellar evolution, spawns its own planetary system. The various stars are so far apart, that their distance must be measured in light years. One light year is the distance light travels in one year, at a speed of 186,000 miles per second.

As stars evolve, from a Red Dwarf of immense density and heat, to a White Giant that is mostly gas and that has only a small percentage of the heat of a new star, a process that takes many billions of years, there is a period somewhere in the middle of this long period when planets are formed by solar explosions. Over millions of years, the planets evolve transient life, as the surfaces gradually cool and water vapor and carbon and the other chemical elements mix and combine and evolve into various plant and animal life forms. George Gamov gives an extensive description of stellar evolution in his classic book *The Birth and Death Of The Sun.* I read it over forty years ago. I was about thirteen at the time, and at first, it upset me to think that our wonderful planet would someday become obsolete.

Most astronomers and physicists ascribe to the theory of the Big Bang. I don't know what the dogs or the porpoises believe, metaphysically speaking. Porpoises have brains that are larger in proportion to their bodies than humans do. Dogs are so smart in the olfactory dimension that they make humans look like moronic amoeba, even though we can smell too.

In the Big Bang theory of the origin of the universe, all matter was originally compressed into such great density that it occupied only a tiny point of space, and then it exploded with such force that it has continued to expand for all time, and the explosion, presumably, continues at the point of origin, resulting in an ever expanding universe. Though I don't understand their math, the scientists have somehow concluded that our location in the continuing explosion is somewhere in the middle.

Logically, I presume that other solar systems that are also somewhere in the middle, given similar physical circumstances (chemical elements, solar and planetary evolution, biological evolution), would have developed civilizations and societies not terribly unlike our own. Given the billions of stars and their solar systems of planets, this conclusion is not only not amazing, it is elementary and obvious, despite what your Granny might think.

In the context of the universe, the civilizations located somewhere in the middle of the expanding universe are relatively primitive and savage. The planetary systems that have evolved much, much longer than those in the middle, those on the outer edge of the expanding universe, are likely to be considerably more evolved, biologically, culturally and philosophically, than we. I do not think that the hypotheses that aliens exist who are far superior to us is remotely far fetched. The universe is *much* bigger than my imagination or yours. If logic has any objective value whatsoever, it is no great leap to assume that there are many aliens in the vast universe who are far, far superior in their evolutionary status to us violent, greedy, dull-witted humans.

We are also capable of love, self-sacrifice, moral integrity, spiritual awareness, altruism, music, art, poetry and heroism. Hopefully, we will evolve in the direction of more of the goodness and less of the evil that are both evident in our nature.

It seems to me that our survival is dependent on our

social and moral evolution. Wouldn't this also be true of a superior alien race? We have wasted too much time arguing about *whether* aliens exist, and as a result, we have not seriously explored the probable nature of superior aliens. I assume that the alligators, one of the oldest species on our planet, devote little or no time to considering *our* superior nature, either, though some of them may have developed a taste for our flesh.

Once a species has evolved to the point where it has threatened the very planet that spawned it, certain social and moral developments, based in mutual love and cooperation, must necessarily evolve in order for that species, and that planet, to continue. We certainly have the physical capacity to blow our own planet to smithereens. Do we also have the capacity to end war and terror and competition and racial and cultural hatred, for the sake of the survival of our species? One prerequisite for our survival is certainly the development of an universal perspective.

Let's think some more about those wonderful aliens. What do you suppose they think of us? Given our own development of technology that allows us to see far into space, a technology that is undoubtedly primitive by comparison to that of a species much more ancient and highly evolved than ours, wouldn't it be logical to assume that these superior, highly evolved aliens are quite capable of monitoring our social and moral development? Would they be as confused as we are about the purposes and priorities of life? Wouldn't they have conquered crime and war and other social ills? It seems to me that their civilizations must be what we would call utopian. If we can *conceive* of utopia, wouldn't a superior species be able to *attain* it?

These are serious questions. There was a time, not long ago, in our short history, that Copernicus was considered a nut case for *informing* us that the Earth revolved around the sun. We thought it would be better to revile him and persecute him, at the time, than to stretch our imaginations ever so little to consider the truth. One man's vision is another man's joke.

We need to reconsider the nature of intelligence. Up to this point, we have steadfastly limited our definition of intelligence to human perception. We must go beyond this anthrocentrism, to consider intelligence in light of adaptability and varied dimensionality.

An eagle has telescopic vision. He can see much more acutely than we can. Even with our binoculars we do not begin to see what an eagle can see, being biologically connected as he is, between vision and brain. Yet, we both 'see'. Our mutual participation in a visual dimension has some areas of overlap. We can only appreciate that which our perceptual ability will reveal to us. Does this mean that, given an expanded visual dimension compared to ours, that the eagle *appreciates* what he sees more than we do? He *sees more* than we do.

As mentioned previously, a dog exists in an olfactory dimension that is far more complex than our own. (He also hears approximately ten times better than we do.) How can we say that we are more intelligent than a dog, given his superiority to us in the olfactory and auditory dimensions? It's doubtful that dogs have much appreciation of Picasso, however, although some dogs seem to enjoy watching television. Maybe they aren't so smart, after all?

I could go on with numerous examples of areas where 'animals' are superior to humans, and it would be fun and even funny, but, enough is enough. I would like to point out, however, that Galapagos Tortoises live to be 300 years old. Do age and wisdom always correlate?

Would highly-evolved, superior aliens consider us in the same way that we consider the other animals, plants and numerous life-forms with whom we 'share' this planet? Maybe they'd take the attitude of *Star Trek* and restrain themselves from interference in alien 'worlds' like ours. If they have a respect for the evolutionary process, they might look but not touch. Maybe they have the capacity to contact us, but do not do so because we have not evolved beyond war, violence and racial and cultural divisiveness. Maybe they do not place a great value on technology, the way we do. Maybe they have *moral standards* to which we give only lip service.

I imagine that in the infinite history of the universe, there have been many, many species who developed the technology to blow themselves up, and did so. They probably had literature, art and music too. They too, had both visionaries and reactionaries that engaged in debates that were never conclusively resolved. And then they died. All of them. And the innocent too. The animals, the plants, the children, those who prayed and those who cared. Perhaps that's where the Black Holes in space came from. Gone is gone, so we'll probably never know. But it seems logical to assume that stupidity and self-destruction are as universal as love. We had to get it from somewhere.

Einstein postulated that energy is constant in the universe, and that it cannot be destroyed, but can only change form. Is there an oversoul of pure energy in the universe, or is it more likely that my finite imagination is greater than all the possibilities in the immense, expanding, ancient universe? Personally, I don't think any human is that smart. But I'm smart enough to know that I don't belong to the most intelligent species in the universe.

If humans are so smart, then why have they

traditionally questioned whether or not other animals actually think and feel? Why are loons more faithful to their spouses than humans? They mate for life, as many 'animals' do. In order to expand your consciousness to develop a universal perspective, anthrocentrism must be left behind. In terms of adaptability, our dogs are smarter than we are. We work all week, for years on end, often at meaningless occupations, to support them. We feed them and house them, and all we ask of them is that they be good dogs. In other words, we ask that they be good at being what they naturally are. Just who is the 'pet' and who the 'master'? You may find this amusing, which it is, but it is also a serious truth. Which of the two species has the higher quality of life?

It is a mark of just how incredibly anthrocentric our species has been that it is only recently that animals have been recognized as having feelings. As a species, we are certainly full of ourselves. No wonder that we can't even get along with each other. Our ethnocentrism is so intense that the common man truly believes that *his* religion is the only true one, not to mention his politics, his country, and his soccer team. Ethnocentric values result in soccer riots of grand proportion, but nobody is rioting for a more equitable distribution of resources to the poor and homeless.

The Christian, the Jew and the Islamic all believe that God is on their side. Wouldn't God be on 'the side' of everyone, including other species? Ethnocentrism is cultural narcissism. Anthrocentrism is species-wide narcissism. Perhaps the aliens from outer space who watch us secretly will consider us savages as long as we fight among ourselves and treat other species as if they are inferior to us. You may find this preposterous, but reality is not limited by your lack of logic and imagination. Every primitive tribe considers itself the center of the universe. How many actual centers of the universe can there be?

Because we have greater direct experience of dogs than any other species, let's continue to compare ourselves to them. Dogs are more sociable than humans. While there are a few heroic humans who will sacrifice themselves for their fellows, every dog will defend his pack to the death, no matter what the odds. Dogs don't tolerate being alone as well as humans. They are happiest when they are in a pack, and can readily adapt to a human family for this purpose. They are more loyal in their relationships than we are, although it would be a toss-up as to which species is more sexually promiscuous.

Dogs do not commit murders of other dogs. Once they establish dominance, they are satisfied. Both species steal. Humans abuse their children at a much greater frequency than dogs do. The average dog is capable of learning 300 to 500 human words. While 50% of Americans "own" a dog, only a few simple words of dog body language are understood. Dogs save human lives so often that it is commonplace news. A day does not go by that some newspaper or broadcast does not report that a dog saved a family from a fire, saved a drowning person or fought off an attacker to save his human 'pet'.

Most people who live with a dog develop true feelings of love for him. If we are observant, we see how responsive dogs are to their environments and experience. We note how happily they greet us and how sad they feel to be left alone. We see how they seem to know when we are hurt or sick, and how they make efforts to comfort us at those times. A cat will do the same thing. Both these 'animals' have individual personalities, as all 'animals' do. Is it such a stretch to define a 'person' as one who has a distinct personality? This only sounds absurd because we can't even get along with members of our own species.   We prefer to focus on our differences rather than our similarities.

The reason dogs are used for medical research is because their systems, including their brains, are remarkably similar to our own. Dogs generally respond to the same drugs in the same way that humans do. Veterinary medicine has recognized this for well over a century. Animal parents love and protect their offspring, and prepare them for independence.   Every animal wants to continue living. Elephants sense their own approaching death and walk to a common elephant graveyard. A rhinoceros will seek out the source of any smoke he smells and stamp out the fire when he finds it, presumably to save his habitat.

Many animals mate for life and will not take another partner if their's perishes. We like to use a euphemism to describe all this and more. If an animal displays behavior or wisdom, we call it 'instinct'. Perhaps it would be fairer to say that each animal, including man, is intelligent *in his own way*. In other words, *intelligence is relative* to adaption and sensory perception.

Few of us are divergent enough in our thinking to consider that the fact that we create technology, which damages the environment and threatens our own survival as a species, is not evidence of our superiority to other animals, but rather of our inferiority to them!   Hypocrisy is an uniquely human trait. We like to give lip service to having 'a reverence for all life' while wolfing down hamburgers, dressing in clothes produced by exploited 'foreign' children in sweatshops, polluting the air burning dwindling fossil fuels in our cars, creating tons of plastic, non-biodegradable trash a day, and hating anyone who doesn't share our spiritual views.

We like to go into a church and compare outfits. We

see no conflict in proclaiming ourselves to be great Christians while devoting our working days to foreclosing and evicting families from their farms. Once in a while, a dog might bite someone who frightens or seems to threaten him or his family. When it is to our advantage, we use human standards to compare an animal to ourselves, but when the same basis is used, and the comparison is unfavorable, we say it is absurd, for we humans are the champions of hypocrisy. We want to have our cake and eat it too. We say we care about the future of our planet, while we continue its destruction, hour by hour, complacently oblivious.

It is universal, among human cultures, to have laws for the good of the many, against murder, theft and treason. Marriage is universal too, and funerals. Religion is also seen, universally, in all human cultures. All cultures develop morality. Families are universal. Education is universal. Economy is universal. We all have a desire to sleep safely, raise our children and survive. We all like to play. Balls, houses and bowls are common to all cultures. We all like sports, and a good meal. Fishing is practiced wherever it can be, and most of us are interested in sex.

Minor differences, such as color, notwithstanding, we are all biologically the same. Blood is blood, and hearts are the same, all over the world.

I pollute the world daily for I am a human hypocrite. I make tons of trash. I drive a car. I call people whom I don't even know rude names. Sometimes I'm inconsiderate to the feelings of others. Sometimes I'm impatient, mean and stupid. Few of us are very good at practicing what we preach. Some of us try to fight our own negative tendencies, and some give in to them. I have helped save a few lives, though. And I've helped a few hundred children, some. In the final count, I hope I come out on the plus side. At least I think

116

about it.

Can the truth set us free? 'To thine own self be true' can be interpreted in two ways. Most interpret it to mean 'to thine own self be loyal'. It also should mean 'to thine own self, *tell the truth*'. Is knowledge power? Does power corrupt? I think that the power of knowledge is neutral, and whether it is used for good or for evil is dependent on the moral choices we make. I don't think there is anything more powerful than death and love, but I wouldn't underestimate the power of greed and hatred.

The credo of the materialist is that "whoever has the most stuff at the end, wins". I have seen it displayed on their bumpers, as if it were funny. Such a belief is beneath contempt. I know it is an attempt at ironic humor, but, sadly, I also know that this is the meaning of life to many millions of people. I would like to assert the opposite: whoever has had the most peak experiences at the end, should be grateful. A peak experience does not come from owning anything. The temporary satisfaction that one might feel by gaining wealth or some desired object is nothing compared to a peak emotional experience, in which you feel the power of love.

I have felt it when I participated in saving someone from drowning, when I know that he was truly in danger before we rescued him, and would have surely died had we not. I also learned the deep disappointment one feels when he fails to rescue someone, and you find him dead in the water. I went into the Coast Guard directly out of high school, and it was the best kind of education for a young man, because it established in me an emotional connection to the lives and deaths of other people.

I have had peak experiences as a teacher, teaching creative writing to gifted and talented teens. There were days when the poetry flowed between us, as we collaborated on

117

group poems, and when I drove home after class, my whole chest was filled with love, hope and gratitude. I have felt it as a guitar player in a rock band, when a song felt just right, and we all clicked perfectly and the blend of instruments was perfectly in sync and transported us all emotionally. I have felt it after long, grueling therapy sessions with families, couples and adolescents, when it had been touch and go, and rough going, but we'd somehow gotten past it and at the end, everyone felt closer, and better, and again, my own chest was filled with love, hope and gratitude.

I've felt it when I've watched my three children being born. The pure rush of love was nearly overwhelming to me at those births. And sometimes, I *have* been overwhelmed, and I've cried tears of joy. I do not hide from joy.

There is no mistaking a peak experience with anything else. I hope you have had many of them. This is what I call quality of life. It's when you breathe easy, and your eyes open all the way, and you feel the total joy of life, grateful, and full of love and hope, that you are really living, feeling perfectly satisfied.

Are these peak experiences mere accidents? Do they have to be few and far between? Or, are they simply the wages of your own ability to live and love? How often could a person feel fully satisfied? Is there a limit to love? The ability to feel the joy of life is a matter of personal capacity. You need to exercise it, in order for your capacity to expand.

We do not know how long our lives will be, but we can make them full. We each have the choice, every day, of living as if that day was our last. How do you know that it isn't?

The reality of death is perfect. If you stay aware of it, you will not waste your time. Time is all you really have. This is the essence of life. This is what really matters, not your retirement account, or your car, or your golf score. Do your children know that you love them? Did you make today Thanksgiving? Did you notice how beautiful the sky looks today? Did you sing a song this morning? Have you let yourself feel satisfied today? How do you feel, *right now?*

The world is not what you make it. The universe is the world, and you are but a small part of it. You can drink from the stream of love, or go thirsty. You can dump new, clean water into the stream, or pollute it.

I believe that each of us is responsible for the world. I believe that love is the positive principle of the universe, the essence of energy and the reason there is something instead of nothing. I believe that each living thing has the energy of love in it. I believe that God *is* love. The material world is ever changing, and temporary. Love never changes. It is the same now as it has ever been, and will be as long as there is life in the universe.

About The Author

Eric Greinke is a veteran of the U.S. Coast Guard, Vietnam Era. He has B.A. Degrees in English (1971) and Psychology (Sociology minor, 1976) and a Masters Degree in Clinical Social Work (1981), Grand Valley State University. He is a Certified Social Worker in the State of Michigan. He has worked with emotionally disturbed and developmentally disabled children for over twenty-five years. He taught creative writing on the secondary level to gifted and talented students prior to becoming a professional social worker.

Mr. Greinke is the author of several books of poetry, social commentary and fiction. He is an avid fisherman and has earned numerous Master Angler awards. He is also a musician who has played in several folk, rock and blues groups over the years.

He has a wife, Roseanne, who is also a professional social worker. His children are Kris (23), Anna (14) and Karl (12). The family dog is Honey, a Pekingese.

Whole Self / Whole World has gone through numerous rewrites over a twenty-seven year period since it was first conceived. Mr. Greinke is currently at work on a collection of children's poems, *Worms Are Delicious*. His novels, *Harry All Over*, *Elephant's Graveyard* and *Sea Dog* are at various stages in the marketing process.